Leadership fo  , Volume IV

Roots for Change:
Grounding Processes of Peacebuilding

**By students in JPST 365 Leadership for Social Justice
Fall 2017 at the University of St. Thomas
Edited by Dr. Mike Klein**

ISBN 10: 1986902641
ISBN 13: 978-1986902649
Order at: https://www.createspace.com/8291295

Cover art by Bridget Carey
Cover design by Sunita Dharod

Table of Contents

Acknowledgements

Student authors would like to express our thanks to:

Sarah Borger, Sexual Violence Center
Eric Boustead, Line Break Media
Norm Champ, Tree Trust
Dave Colling, Harrison Neighborhood Association
Janet Curiel
Elena Dahlberg, Urban Strategies
Allison Johnson Heist, Headwaters Foundation
Alexandra Spieldoch and Don Jacobson, Compatible Technologies
International
Ian Kantonen, MPIRG
Dana Mortenson, World Savvy
Eric Neisheim, Minnesota Literacy Council
Dung Phan, Vietnamese Social Service of Minnesota
…and to our professor, Mike Klein

Introduction to Leadership Profiles

The leadership profiles collected in this volume are generated from the work of undergraduate students in a course entitled Leadership for Social Justice. As a writing-intensive course in the Department of Justice and Peace Studies at the University of St. Thomas, Minnesota, USA, students compose profiles over the course of a semester framed by five assignments (see Pedagogy below). Each of the profiles follows a common format: story, theory, collective action, biography, and references. These stories describe leadership for social justice and peacebuilding, all terms that require some description.

Our approach to leadership is not based on positional or individual leadership, as is so often the presumption of leadership theory that focuses on traits or characteristics. Instead leadership is described in the course (and in detail below) as the dynamics of power, operating between individuals with different identities and with differential agency to affect change. These profiles do not ignore the role of individual leaders enacting power. Instead, the individual is de-centered to refine the focus on how power operates in the relationships between individuals, groups, and systems.

Social justice is the ability for people to participate in the decisions that most affect their lives. It is defined by recognition of rights and responsibilities in an organization, community, or society, and by distribution of income and wealth such that everyone has the opportunity to live and thrive. Peacebuilding is the structural work to create the conditions for social justice. In the field of peace studies, peace is defined as the absence of violent conflict (negative peace), and as the presence of just relationships and systems to deal with conflict nonviolently and promote human flourishing (positive peace). Peacebuilding is proactive work to develop the structures that support positive peace, prevent violent conflict, and increase human agency.

Students chose the title *Roots for Change: Grounding Processes of Peacebuilding* to describe their collected work. They tell stories of peacebuilding grounded in local neighborhood contexts and in solidarity with global movements. They profile courageous individual organizers and organizations. Students write to re-present voices authentically, and describe peacebuilding responsibly, hoping they will encourage and inspire you, reader, to enact your own leadership for social justice.

As their professor and editor, I hope this volume provides an opportunity for students to enact their own learning, and to advance their own leadership. I am proud of their work and hopeful for the world you, me, and humanity will build together in the pursuit of peace.

Pedagogy

The profiles collected here provide diverse and remarkable accounts of leadership for social justice. They also represent the work of students in the Leadership for Social Justice course in the Department of Justice and Peace Studies at the University of St. Thomas in Saint Paul, Minnesota, USA. Several pedagogical elements of this course are foundational to the profiles presented above and are described here to add context to the process underlying this text.

Writing in the Disciplines

Under an institutional Writing Across the Curriculum (WAC) program, Writing in the Disciplines projects are founded on specialized skills student develop in order to write effectively in different academic disciplines and associated professions. Each assignment encourages students to practice writing in formats that reflect the discipline and prepare them for professional writing. It is product-driven approach to learning that sets a high bar for student achievement. In particular, this assignment calls on students to be ethical and authentic in their representation of the voices of their profile subject. They must also be responsible for a profile that is published and publicly available, and accountable to the subject of their profile. Students must achieve a minimum standard of quality, reflected through their course grade, to be included in this publication. Student research was approved by the University of St. Thomas Institutional Review Board (IRB# 819449-3).

The Circle of Praxis

This pedagogical model is based on the work of Brazilian educator Paulo Freire. As a literacy educator in Brazil, Freire developed a praxis approach to education that went beyond knowledge to empower students for liberation from oppressive systems. This methodology is presented in Freire's *Pedagogy of the Oppressed* (1970) and subsequent works (1973, 1985, 1998), and further developed in liberation theology (Guttierez, 1988; Ellacuria & Sobrino, 1993). A particular form of praxis pedagogy, the Circle of Praxis (Smith & Haasl, 1999), is central to my own research and teaching (Klein, 2013, 2016). The Circle of Praxis is a concise yet expansive approach to education that informs the course that generated this text.

The Circle of Praxis is made up of four broad educational steps. This methodology begins in the *experience of injustice*, starting from the margins of power, and in solidarity with people subject to oppression. Experience may be direct or vicarious through first-hand accounts, primary sources, or other media, like this text. In the second step, experience is subjected to *descriptive analysis* through the social sciences, especially history, sociology, economics and political science. In the third step, descriptions are interpreted through *normative analysis* to examine worldviews, religious perspectives, assumptions, and constructions of meaning that describe power differentials and promote ethical collective agency to make change. The fourth step, *action planning*, develops strategies that promote justice and peace, and tactics that account for available resources, potential obstacles, allies and adversaries. And this last step leads to the next experience in the cycle.

Courses in the Department of Justice and Peace Studies are framed by Circle of Praxis pedagogy. Leadership for Social Justice is grounded in the stories of people facing injustice and oppression in order to see empathetically (if imperfectly) from that perspective. Then descriptive and normative analyses provide understanding for action planning. Our goal is not just to know the world, but also to act in the world to advance common goods.

Social Change Wheel

Social change wheel models describe complementary strategies in work for social justice. The earliest social change wheel model seems to have been developed by Langseth and Troppe in (1996), and then published by the same authors a year later (1997). Social change wheel adaptations can be found at the University of Minnesota, College of St. Benedict,  and the University of St. Thomas. These adaptations typically reference Langseth and Troppe, or Minnesota Campus Compact, which has since updated its own model in a more detailed form.

The Langseth and Troppe social change wheel was originally composed of six categories around an empty hub: *Charitable Volunteerism, Community/Economic Development, Voting/Formal Political Activities, Confrontational Strategies, Grassroots Political Activity/Public Policy Work,* and *Community Building* (Minnesota Campus Compact, 1997). My own adaptation of this model adds the category *education* in the hub or center of the wheel (Klein, 2017).

Because the other categories of the social change wheel rely on knowledge or skills in order to be effective, education - in the form of teaching, learning, training, or awareness - is a significant foundation for the other six categories and an important node of connection between them.

Of course, these categories may overlap when applied to real situations. For example, *public policy* is sometimes formulated within the context of *grassroots organizing* and shaped by lawmakers within *formal political activities*. And social change wheel categories could be further defined and elaborated. For example, *confrontational strategies* could be expanded into Gene Sharp's 198 methods of nonviolent direct action (1973). And categories are somewhat arbitrarily ordered on the wheel; the model does not imply movement from one category to the next in ordered rotation, so much as a web of relationships between categories, often (but not always) intersecting through education.

Social change wheels also help identify relationships between different methods of change: concurrent or sequential strategies, complementary or supportive strategies, and the potential of employing several strategies rather than single approaches to justice work. Thus, *charitable volunteerism* can be appreciated not just for its own sake, but also for supporting other strategies by extending immediate support in the midst of long-term change. Social change wheels can also suggest the limitations of any one strategy, if it is not connected to other methods of justice work.

These are the primary pedagogical models for the course Leadership for Social Justice. Other theories and concepts are represented in each profile's work and references, and in the bibliography and index at the end of the book.

Works Cited

Ellacuria, I. & Sobrino, J. (1993). Mysterium liberationis: Fundamental   concepts of liberation theology. Maryknoll, NY: Orbis

Freire, P. (1970/1990). Pedagogy of the oppressed. New York: Continuum.

_____. (1973). Education for critical consciousness. New York: Continuum.

_____. (1985). The politics of education: Culture, power, and liberation. New York: Bergin & Garvey.

_____. (1998). Pedagogy of freedom: Ethics, democracy, and civic courage. Lanham, MD: Rowman & Littlefield.

Gutierrez, G., (1988). A theology of liberation: History, politics, and salvation. Maryknoll, N.Y: Orbis Books.

Klein, Mike. (2013). "Cell phones, T-shirts and Coffee: Codification of Commodities in a Circle of Praxis Pedagogy." *Peace Studies Journal Special Edition: The Business of War and Peace, and the Potential for Education to Play a Transformative Role*, 6(1) 31-45.

Klein, Mike. (2016). *Democratizing Leadership: Counter-Hegemonic Democracy in Communities, Organizations, and Institutions*. Vol. 1 of Counter-Hegemonic Democracy and Social Change. Charlotte, NC: Information Age Publishing.

Klein, M. (2017). Social change wheel analysis: Beyond the dichotomy of charity or justice, in Colon, C.; Gristwood, A. & Woolf, M. (2017). *Civil Rights and Inequalities, Occasional Publication #6*, Boston: CAPA, The Global Education Network.

Langseth, M. & Troppe, M. (1997). So what? Does service-learning really foster social change? Expanding boundaries: Building civic responsibility within higher education, 2, 37-42

Smith, David. W. & Haasl, Mike. (1999). "Justice and Peace Studies at the University of St. Thomas", In Weigart, Kathleen M., Crews, Robin J. *Teaching for justice: Concepts and Models for Service-learning in Peace Studies*. Washington, D.C: American Association for Higher Education

Sharp, G. (1973). *The politics of nonviolent action / Gene Sharp ; with the editorial assistance of Marina Finkelstein*. (Extending horizons books). Boston: P. Sargent Publisher.

Climate Generation: A Will Steger Legacy
Katy Struntz

Story

Over the course of 50 years, Will Steger has led record and ground-breaking dogsled expeditions in the arctic regions of our earth. He has seen firsthand how humans are impacting the environment; glaciers and ice shelfs have melted and shrunk before his eyes, landscapes he had come to know on his expeditions were almost completely different when he returned. Will Steger's experiences had such a profound effect on him that he went home and started a foundation to raise awareness and educate people on what was happening in the arctic regions and why.

What started in 2006 as the Will Steger Foundation was re-named Climate Generation: a Will Steger Legacy in 2014. It was created with the mission to educate and empower people on all things climate change. He used his unique, firsthand experience to inform others and his background in education to start designing a curriculum. Since its founding Climate Generation, a nonprofit organization, has formed a board of directors, an advisory board, created a team of employees, and found support in many volunteers. Pulling from a diverse range of backgrounds, Climate Generation is supported, advised, and facilitated by people who have come together through their shared interest in educating and finding solutions to climate change. The board of directors offers strategic vision and direction, as well as helps finance

Climate Generation. The advisory board is made up of respected individuals who have an active relationship with Climate Generation, and who are making contributions in the area of climate change, renewable energy, philanthropy, and policy. The advisory board also serves as an important community champion for Climate Generation, using their resources and mission to engage their communities in climate change solutions. A broad range of skillsets keep Climate Generation moving in an effective direction. Engineers, scientists, educators from the University of St. Thomas and the University of Minnesota, entrepreneurs, local businesses, former policy makers, lawyers, decision makers from Xcel Energy as well as people with experience in marketing, communications, and non-profit organizations make up Climate Generation's upper level positions.

Climate Generation also has an in-house team that is comprised of people in charge of media engagement, program directors, communication, education, and youth programs. These people are instrumental in education and youth engagement. Climate Generation would be able to reach as many people as they do or helped push Minnesota towards greener policy without the this help of these individuals. So many people from so many backgrounds effectively communicating and working together is crucial for the organizations continuing work and success.

Through their work, Climate Generation has come to realize that equitable solutions cannot be found by following a science and policy method alone. An organization made up of primarily white employees, directors, and advisors, climate change looks and feels differently to them than it does to people in different cultural, economic, and social groups. They have committed themselves to addressing how climate change intersects with economic, racial, and social disparities. Some of the ways they're going about this is by addressing their position compared to others, undergoing trainings on racism and the role of environmental justice, and engage environmental justice partners as equals while taking into consideration their time, history and expertise.

Climate Generation has a lot of resources and opportunities for everyone to get involved like their core youth directed programs, curriculum, mentorship programs, and professional development courses for educators. YEA! MN, Youth Environmental Activists Minnesota, is one of their youth programs that empowers high school students to own their power and take coordinated action to ensure an equitable transition to a healthier climate future. It supports high school students all over the Twin Cities metro area who are trying to create change in their own communities. YEA! MN does not have a set path for students to follow, it is a tool for students to use as they begin their environmental work. If students aren't sure where to start, have a project that needs support, or need help starting a club at school, YEA! MN can step in and help at any stage. They support and empower, they do not push and control.

From its founding ten years ago, Climate Generation has reached thousands of people, they have grown their networks around the Midwest, are gaining more and more public attention, and are helping connect youth with climate leaders and organizations all with the goal of creating equitable solutions for climate change.

Theory

Behind every movement stands a collection of people because, as we know, nothing is accomplished alone. Social justice leaders know that there is a network of people - a web of relationships - that creates momentum and fosters creative problem solving. What makes an organization like Climate Generation: A Will Steger Legacy thrive? How are they continually reaching more and more people? And how have they been instrumental in green solutions and climate education in the Midwest area? By building and fostering their web of relationships.

John Paul Lederach realized that the relationships behind people and organizations are key elements in successful social change, and if those relationships collapse social change will not hold (Lederach, 2005). Using spider webs as a metaphor, Lederach describes the growth of the web and how each point of interaction serves a purpose, to create the frame, to strengthen, and to solidify (2005). Once a web has been started, and relational spaces have been created, a space for creativity and social energy emerges, and when that energy needs to be refocused and directed, the center of the web is where people can return (Lederach, 2005). Like spider webs, relational webs serve the same purpose with every point of interaction and every new strand building and strengthening the social movement (Lederach, 2005). For Climate Generation, the base of their web starts with their founder, Will Steger. From him, the web grows through the board of directors, to the advisory board, the in-house staff, volunteers, and the thousands of people they have reached throughout the Midwest region.

Climate Generation's web consists of people from all kinds of backgrounds and skill sets, each bringing something unique to the organization. This wide array of skills and knowledge creates a necessary network for their continuing success and progression towards social change. People with backgrounds in marketing, communications, finance, and nonprofits lend direction and advise on how to run the organization itself. Educators that help implement and build curricula. Business people and previous policy makers help navigate the corporate and political aspects of enacting social change. They can also serve as mentors for younger people and help guide them through the nuances of climate change that they have encountered or may understand better. These are some of the first strands in the web, building a network that pulls in people with different backgrounds who have similar goals. Building a strong foundation helps keep the center from collapsing.

The relationships and creative space created by these people have led to educational programs and professional development that reaches 5,000 educators a year (Our Impact, 2017), youth programs that reach out to many high schools and hundreds of youth, and partnerships with local businesses and government institutions. By connecting with more and more people, and by creating partnerships with other institutions, the goals of Climate Generation have places to spread to and gain momentum as well as find support.

Climate Generation is also the center that people can go back to when they need direction. Connected with twenty-five high schools, their YEA! MN program helps guide and support students while leaving enough space for them to work through problems and come up with solutions for themselves and their clubs (Our Impact, 2017). Climate Generation acts as the center of the web for students, giving them a place to come back to for direction and focus when they need it. Helping students at such an early stage in their journey gives them a broader range of tools to use in talking about and creating solutions for climate change. They will continue to use these tools as they get older and enter new communities, spreading their network and working towards justice in more than one area.

However, it isn't enough to create webs full of the same types of people. To enact constructive change, some relations need to be formed with people who are not necessarily like-minded or like-situated (Lederach, 85). As a predominately middle class, white organization, their solutions to climate change are not the same as people in different cultural, economic, or social situations, and so Climate Generation must take this into account when moving forward with their vision. In acknowledging this, Climate Generation is not only expanding its web of relations, it's opening up new doors to go about solving climate change and diversifying the approaches we can all take.

A web of relationships is crucial for social movements in advancing and enacting change. They serve as places for creativity to thrive, and as a base for direction and focus. They unite people from different backgrounds in a common goal or interest. Finally, they help spread the change even further, as one person connects with another and that person connects with another, and so on. Climate Generation is continually building its web, pulling in more and more people from different communities and different backgrounds. Not only does this strengthen their support system, it offers new ideas and perspectives that can generate more creativity and different approaches to finding equitable solutions to climate change. Without support, and without building relationships with people who come from different backgrounds, social change will not flourish. The will of the masses determines change, so the bigger the web the better.

Action Planning

A SWOT analysis can be a useful tool for any organization that wishes to assess their strengths, weaknesses, opportunities, and threats to advancement. By analyzing and addressing these different aspects, action for progress and growth can strengthen the organization and keep it moving forward as well as tackle any problems or obstacles getting in the way of progress.

The strengths of Climate Generation are easy to see. They have a solid foundation of directors, advisees, and internal staff. With so many skillsets and educational backgrounds, problems and solutions can be approached from a multidimensional approach creating the best possible outcomes. It also offers a wide array of viewpoints and opinions about how Climate Generation could be improved, like their renewed mission of working with and understanding climate change from diverse viewpoints other than their own.

In a culture that demands evidence and facts, Will Steger's firsthand experience of climate change is invaluable in connecting and educating people. He still gets invited to speak about his time in the arctic and the melting of our polar icecaps, for instance he was invited to the University of St. Thomas last year which is how I became aware of Climate Generation.

The curriculum is packed full of information from the leading scientific agencies (such as NASA) and partners with Minnesota educational boards to ensure that accurate information is being spread, giving educators the best possible information to relay to students. Their youth programs go beyond educating, building skills needed for effectively communicating about climate change, using problem solving skills to come up with solutions to climate change, and developing leadership skills to implement these solutions in their communities.

As with any organization, weaknesses can be found. As shown

before, the web of relationships is a key part of how Climate Generation operates and works towards social justice. But some weakness may be found in their network. As made evident by Climate Generation itself, it is a predominately white organization that reaches predominately white groups. To fully understand how climate change affects everyone and how to create solutions that are equitable for everyone, including more diverse voices and perspectives, Climate Generation needs to not only address this, but actively work towards understanding these differences.

They have a strong base of support from people who view climate change the same way. While this is important, it is equally important to build a network with others so that Climate Generation's mission towards climate and social justice may be realized by even more people. Connecting with different groups builds another level of support. Without building these networks, Climate Generation risks losing momentum and plateauing their efforts.

Even so, Climate Generation still has promising opportunities to advance their mission. The thousands of educators they reach through their curriculum and professional development courses reach out to even more people, creating a sort of indirect network of people who learn about climate change, it's consequences, and what can be done to prevent these consequences. The more people reached, the bigger the impact.

Another opportunity for advancing Climate Generation's mission are the students they are reaching. These young people are learning important skills on how to problem solve, communicate, and mobilize their own communities. Through all of this, Climate Generation is solidifying the importance and significance of climate change and solutions for it in young people who will soon enough be making big decisions that can help turn around the current way of doing things. And on the way, they can start with their communities, which is as important as big structural change.

There are of course, always threats to progress. Big or small, these can get in the way of an organization's mission. For Climate

Generation, one threat is mental exhaustion and hopelessness. In the current political and social climate, amplified by social media and our constant access to information, it is very easy to be worn down. With the seemingly constant headlines of how climate change is getting worse or how our current administration continues to deny and contribute to climate change there is a risk of people losing steam and stopping their advocacy work. This also means that people Climate Generation could have potentially reached, may not be as open to fighting what seems like an un-winnable fight.

Optimism and the endurance to keep fighting is important for keeping Climate Generation's vision alive and to keep spreading their mission to others. It's important that Climate Generation not only addresses the negative things happening, but also the positive things: reminding people that ending climate change is on a lot of people's minds and collective action will instill change. Structural change seems daunting, but it can be accomplished if enough people join in the fight. And while Climate Generation needs to be aware of threats to their mission, they should also connect with people and organizations unlike themselves. This will help them build their network in a way that reaches more types of people, thus spreading their mission even further.

Using the SWOT analysis shows us that while Climate Generation is more successful each year, there are ways they can expand and things they can address to keep thriving and keep spreading their mission. Climate justice that is equitable for all is possible, and Climate Generation is working to see that this happens. But how to go about creating these connections is a challenge. How do you connect on a deeper level with people who have different beliefs than you do? How do you keep this connection and how do you show them why your side is the 'right' side? With something like climate change, backed with science and hard evidence, it seems like this should be easy. And yet, there are still a lot of people who either don't believe in it or place more value in faceless corporations that continue to rob the poor and pollute the earth. And how do you find time and strategies to keep from burning out or falling victim to the tireless headlines stating that our earth is doomed?

It is my hope that Climate Generation finds the answers to these questions and figures out how to combat them. I also hope that their education and youth programs keep reaching more and more people, creating educated problem solvers that bring about the structural and social change needed to keep climate change from advancing any more than it already has. In the meantime, I encourage all of you to educate yourselves on the current climate science and think about steps you can take to find equitable solutions to this problem that affects all of us.

Works Cited

Climate Generation: A Will Steger Legacy. (n.d.). Our mission and vision statement. Retrieved from, https://www.climategen.org/who-we-are/our-mission-and-vision/

Lederach, J. P. (2005). *The moral imagination.* New York, NY: Oxford University Press.

About the Author – Katy Struntz

I am currently a psychology major and sustainability minor at the University of St. Thomas. If I had the time and resources, I would major in about five more areas. I'm a serial procrastinator with a lot of ambitious goals but I seem to have found a decent harmony between those two aspects of myself. After graduating I plan on spending a year in South Korea, my country of origin, and from there the plan is to become a trauma counselor. I spend too much money on coffee. I believe we are at an interesting turning point in America where marginalized groups of people are fed up with the quasi-equality we're told we have and I for one cannot wait until our time finally comes, full force.

Compatible Technology International
Bridget M. Carey

Story

The strength of women farmers in Sub-Saharan Africa is awe-inspiring. In the African heat, often with a baby on their backs, women work in the fields to harvest and process crop to feed their families and sell at market. They put in the back-breaking labor necessary by shelling acres of peanuts (or groundnuts) by hand, threshing millet with mortar and pestle, and winnowing with the help of the natural wind and gravity. Despite their incredible dedication, these processes result in an excess amount of drudgery, great loss in crop and low-quality product.

There is a great lack of access to tools in Sub-Saharan Africa causing inefficiencies in food production for laborers, majority of whom are women. It is laborious work unassisted by equipment and results in large food loss in both quantity and quality through the process. Because of the gendered divide in the work, processing food in this way reinforces the lower social and economic status of women as well as the structure of the family. Without more efficient tools, many farmers are kept at an impoverished economic state because of the low market values of their crops.

I was introduced to such women in villages around Thies & Diourbel, Senegal and Lilongwe, Malawi through the stories I heard at Compatible Technology International (CTI). I was an engineering intern through the partnership between CTI and my Peace Engineering Program at University of St Thomas. I've been touched by the farmers' dedication to their work and their passion to accomplish much through their businesses. During my time at CTI, I've seen women beam with pride because not only do they have access to tools that help them do their processing more efficiently, but because they helped design that tool. Compatible Technology is designing tools with subsistent, small-holder farmers to thrive in their own way.

Compatible Technology International was founded by retired food scientist, George Ewing, who had a mission to design tools for the poor, specifically food processing tools. Through his connections at General Mills, he gathered like-minded engineers and scientists to start creating technology for the poor throughout the world that would help them increase their agency. The founders saw the great value of the user's voice in the design process so that the tool could serve users in applicable ways to their own circumstances. In 2014, CTI made an organizational decision to focus their work and service for Sub-Saharan African farmers. In an interview with executive director, Alexandra Spieldoch, said the region was chosen because of its potential capacity and need for post-harvest tools. The regional focus also allowed CTI to commit to a greater relationship with their end-users, allowing their voices to be heard more clearly in the design.

Both my working experience and direct conversations with the executive director provide a testament that CTI is actively seeking effective methods of understanding with farmers. Thus far, and stemming from the organizational decision in 2014, they have been investing in people by hiring African in-country directors and partners that have lived experience with the farming communities. These partners provide "on the ground" knowledge of collaborating villages, the proper engagement practices, and their crops to support the relationship between US CTI staff and farmers. Fostering this positive relationship keeps CTI grounded in their story of self and respects a growing story of us with the farmers.

Theory

Myles Horton describes democracy as "a philosophical concept meaning that people are free and empowered to make collectively the decisions that affect their lives" (Klein, Democratizing Leadership, 2016). Described in Klein's work *Democratizing Leadership*, voice, decision-making, and collective action are three formative and iterative components necessary in democratic societies, actions, and organizations. People in a democratic society are expected to use their voice to influence decision making towards actualizing theirs needs and values. Those decisions are then used to initialize collective action, collaboratively creating something new, such as a stronger organization, a design project, or a movement for social change. Although the three steps may sound straight forward, each require conscientious implementation. Through theorizing CTI's relationship with farmers, we are able to see how use of voice and receptivity to voice can empower farmers to grow their businesses and grow the relationship with CTI to become more democratic. It can also be more broadly examined as the influence of individual and collective voice within peace engineering.

The way CTI reaches out to farmers as "co-designers" resounds with the theory of voice. One way to think about the concept of voice is the expression of your authentic self. How you phrase words to explain your position, your unique artistic interpretations of feelings or situations, or the medium of which you choose to express yourself can all contribute to the complex development of one's voice. Voice has three interwoven parts: Finding voice, using voice, and using voice together (Klein, Democratizing Leadership, 2016). There are ways in which using your voice can help you find your voice, or by using voice together helps you have more confidence in using your own voice. When speaking about the strategies in social justice, CTI's Spieldoch named the need for voice of all working with the organization. She values the expression of one's self and ideas seeing them as a contribution to the mission of CTI.

At the beginning of each project, CTI gathers both quantitative and qualitative information through farmer interviews about need, demand, and contextual information by partnering with soci-economic consultants, gender specialists, and other in-country partners. By recognizing the gendered dynamics that often play out within communities – majority of women doing laborious work while men more often do the technical or financial related work – CTI is able to take a proactive step in allowing women a voice while not excluding the men. Again, we're able to see the benefits of the 2014 organizational decision to move closer to the famers. By having in-country staff and partners, they are able to assess the strengths and needs of all communities more closely as well as amplify the voice of the farmers.

Potentially the most influential time for farmers to use their voice is during interviews about design prototypes. CTI members and partners use active listening techniques to understand their concerns and needs as best they can and are then carried forward into the design decisions. This is comparable to Klein's experience in a community-led art production where, "artists affirming or grounding their idea in individual voices from the community. . . commands priority over extrapolations from within the artists' meetings or altogether new ideas from the artists." (Democratizing Leadership, 2016 p. 250). Extrapolations from participants' expressions of wants or needs have potential for distancing engineers from the community, which would take away from farmers the power/agency of being a co-designer. In direct conversation with Spieldoch, she identified the need to hear farmers to identify the root cause, need, or problem while receiving feedback. Understanding voice on a deeper, authentic level will allow tools to be designed well and farmers to thrive.

CTI models a facet of the growing notion of peace engineering, a diverse field of engineering that uses technical skills to serve societal needs by allowing social analysis to inform decisions. Peace

Engineering is gaining popularity because of the recognized need for technology in peacebuilding within areas of direct violent conflict. However, peacebuilding is needed in areas experiencing negative peace, the absence of violence without the attendant development of justice. The idea of negative peace is coupled with positive peace in which all forms all violence – direct, structural, and cultural – are absent (Galtung, "An Editorial", 1964). Peace engineering transforms negative peace with pervading injustices towards a more positive peace. By engaging with the user and allowing them to be "co-designers", CTI challenges distributive injustices such as poverty in a sustainable manner and thereby participates in the development of voice in those it serves.

Peace Engineering is developing as a way for engineers to engage more directly with society to address design challenges in a greater context. It requires conversation between engineers and those impacted by the design to understand a greater context that will influence the process. CTI is a visible example of this because of their dedication to actively listening to voices across a number of differing cultural, economic, and societal norms. However, it is important to note that peace engineering can happen anywhere, within cultures and smaller shared societies, in pursuit of this creative and collective work. The efficacy of peace engineering within CTI and Sub-Saharan Africa is clear because of the large impact within the communities that use its tools. As a student pioneering her way in this budding field, I appreciate the opportunity to engage in the work that CTI is facilitating. The reciprocal engagement of CTI staff and farmers speaks volumes to the power of voice for collaborative engineering within a particular societal context.

Action Planning

"We've got a lot more work to do. The real possibility is there to be able to scale our work." (Compatible Technology International. 2017). Spieldoch identified the "tool as a catalyst". Once the tool has been designed, it is not the end. The designing process does not encompass the whole relationship with farmers, but it initiates change to gain more access to markets with higher value product. Whether it is grinding millet to flour, shelling peanuts with less containments, or processing harvest crops with less waste, CTI tools could open doors to higher yields, more competitive pricing, and more income for necessary family care. Interconnected relationships are truly necessary to increase the farmer's access to market. We'll explore the growing relationship between farmers, CTI staff, and others surrounding a defined central relationship to find strong connection where collective action can happen, and to identify opportunities for collective action to strengthen connections.

CTI's mission statement to "[help] families in developing countries access innovative farming tools so they can . . . bring their crops to market" defines the central relationship between farmer and buyer. As an organization, CTI's purpose is to strength the business relationship between the supplier and the buyer through distribution of tools. The map below shows a simple view of the many contributors to this central relationship. The lines represent the frequency of interaction, either in-person or via conference call. The darkest color boxes are outside organizations or hires. The grey colored boxes are CTI staff or volunteers. The light boxes are those in-country not directly affiliated with CTI outside of the tool relationship.

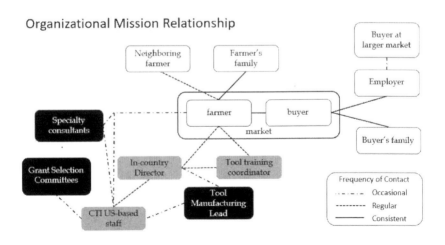

Organizational Mission Relationship

The map shows the strong relationships within CTI and with direct partners. The surrounding relationships, although not as connected directly to CTI, are important to recognize, such as the farmer's family dependent connection to the farmer, or the potentially mutually beneficial neighboring farmers. These relationships are strategically important to acknowledge more opportunities for collective actions. For example, neighboring farmers will often share costs and use of bigger, more expensive tools, such as the thresher. Knowing this relationship, CTI is able to set their price points accordingly.

However, as a peace engineer looking to find more space within the design process for voice, another map would be useful. The in-country director is a spokesperson for the farming communities, often relying heavily upon their expression of voice. By shifting the central relationship to the farmer and In-country Director, we are able to focus on the relationship dynamics specifically during the design process.

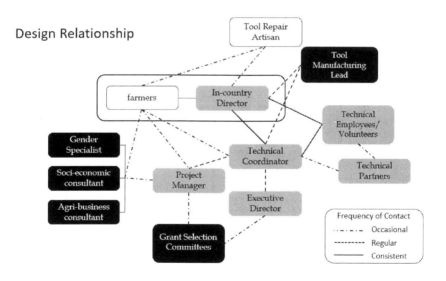

Design Relationship

Use of collective voice relies heavily on the nature of the relationship between farmer and in-country director as well as the group of specialist researchers at the beginning of a project. However, having only one point of contact for the length of the project to represent many communities could be strenuous, for both the director and the project. The process may benefit from multiple voices to provide more perspectives from diverse farmers at different points in the process, and to consistently hear the voice of the farmer.

Another consideration during the design process is the way in which the multiple technical advisers to the US CTI design team hear the voice of the farmer. The In-country Director, again, often provides the "grounding", intentional focus on farmer experience and voice, in design meetings, but how might technical partners, volunteers, and employees hear more authentically and consistently the voice of the farmer? Of course, reflective experiences with the farmers would provide greater understanding of their voice, however with partners from corporate companies or university student groups that's not possible. A stronger relationship between the technical coordinator and the farmer, in partnership with the In-country Director, will amplify the voice of the farmer. This may require more frequent visits in-country to gain the skills and trust necessary to share the farmers' stories authentically in design team settings.

Storytelling and the active listening could also be effective ways reflect farmers' voices to technical partners. Storytelling has the power to communicate the meaning of lived experiences to those who would otherwise not have access. Therefore, a purposeful story to contextualize design meetings could be another way to connect technical partners and farmers. As previously mentioned, active listening is a method that peace engineers could develop and contribute to the engineering profession. Using these techniques within design meetings could reflect what's happening in-country during interviews, as well as prepare partners to be more apt to hear farmers' voice throughout the design process.

In my continued work with CTI, I am looking forward to exploring ways of hearing and valuing farmers' voice with our technical partners, particularly by including concepts of peace engineering. As CTI transitions to scaling their work, it will be important to consider how to maintain and strengthen the voice of the farmer by growing and developing structured relationships within the organizational process. The efficacy of their work will depend on the nurturing of democratic relationships with farmers to find, use, and collect their voices to increase farmer access to market.

Works Cited

Compatible Technology International. (May 25, 2017). CTI: Idealists with a pragmatic approach to ending hunger. [Video file]. Retrieved from https://www.youtube.com/watch?v=Ch6r9uD1CCQ

Galtung, Johann (1964). "An Editorial" Journal of Peace Research. 1(1): pp 1-4

Klein, M. (2016). Democratizing leadership counter-hegemonic democracy in organizations, institutions, and communities. Charlotte, NC: Information Age Publishing Inc.

A. Spieldoch, personal communication, October 26, 2017.

About the Author – Bridget M. Carey

I am currently a mechanical engineering student at University of St Thomas pursuing the Peace Engineering Program. Guided by my Catholic faith and commitment to human dignity, I have found a passion for service and creativity. When not in the classroom, you can find me enjoying a good book, movie, or theatre tunes.

The Cultural Wellness Center
Deborah Honore

Cultural Wellness is a practice. To begin to ground yourself in a sense of culture is a way of proving yourself with healing. —Brother Tezet

Story

Racism, what a loaded word. There's no easy way to have a conversation about it. I think that this is especially true today. With the latest Presidential administration and the hateful rhetoric in our society, structural racism has become undeniable. It's such an overwhelming evil. It's also so interwoven in America's existence, and many don't realize just how much they have internalized racism.

The impacts of structural racism don't just impact a system; it impacts the individuals in it. Racism is dehumanizing. When internalized, it reflects the quality of its victim's lives. The Cultural Wellness Center's mission is to fight the internalization of structural racism in an individual and their community. I choose to tell the center's story through my journey of healing the impacts racism has had me. I will go through this process with the help of The Cultural

Wellness Center. This chapter will include an examination of my unconscious understanding of America's racist structure, and my awakening to consciousness.

My Context: In the 2016 Pioneer Press article, *Minnesota's worsening racial disparity: Why it matters to everyone*, it states, "Minnesota has some of the worst racial disparities in the nation — gaps that have widened over the past five decades." I think because Minnesota is a northern state, many people believe that it's the best place for people of color to live. Minnesota's population is nearly 81 percent white, and a significant portion of the 21 percent left are immigrant populations. I grew up in the Twin Cities. My parents and I resettled in Minnesota as refugees in 1997. Escaping civil violence and lack of resources in both Democratic Republic of the Congo and Ethiopia, we set out for the American dream. Two children later, my parents split, and my mother raised us on her own.

Living Unconscious: Growing up in Minnesota I lived in many identities. I learned very fast that my identity depended entirely on the spaces I was in. Depending on where I was, I could only be African, Ethiopian, or Black. Each identity had its package of preconceived notions that an outsider would attach to me. Each identity has a "box" that I was forced to fit in. As I look back, I don't think I ever entirely identified as just African, Ethiopian, or black. I was sort of identity-less for long period of my life, never really fitting in anywhere. I think because of this; I was able to look at my surroundings more critically. Although I didn't realize it then, I was already recognizing impacts of structural racism in my schools, neighborhood, communities, and in my social groups.

Awakening: For change to happen you need conflict. You need to recognize that there is a problem. I started to recognize the impacts of structural racism, my conflict, at a young age. I first recognized it in my education. In 2016 Charles R. "Charlie" Weaver, Jr. wrote an article for the Pioneer Press entitled *Charlie Weaver: Address Minnesota's racial disparities*. Charles Weaver is a Minnesota politician, a former Chief of Staff for Minnesota Governor Tim Pawlenty, a former Commissioner of the Minnesota Department of Public Safety, and a former Minnesota State Representative. In his article, he stated, "Economic and racial disparities in Minnesota are the direct result of an education system that has failed students of color for generations and produced the largest achievement gap in the nation." For a long time, I blamed my peers for their lack of academic achievements. It wasn't until I graduated high school that I realized that students of color are mostly a product of America's flawed, and racist structure.

Not only was there a lack of resources in my schools, but there was also a lack of drive. My black peers never expected much of themselves, and neither did their teachers. My mother raised me to understand that I could be whomever I wanted to be. To do this, I had to work hard. I often found a disconnect with my black classmates when it came to this understanding. Many of my classmates of color would attribute their low grades, and tests scores to their identity. I will never forget the day I asked a friend why he wasn't reading our in-class assignment, and he answered me with, "girl I'm black, I don't read." This was in middle school, and I was astonished. I carried that racialized integration with me throughout my entire academic career. To this young boy, being black meant he couldn't succeed academically, and he wasn't the only one that thought this way. I've had many conversations like this one since.

Maxfield Magnet school, located in the St. Paul Rondo Community, has been struggling with the same problem in their middle school that I faced when I was younger. In 2013 the former principle Nancy Stachel reached out to The Cultural Wellness Center to make a positive change. In an interview about The Culture Wellness Program, Principle Stachel stated,

> That first year we had a huge issue with bullying and I, of course, went to all the technical solutions we do in schools. Which is, you know, if you do this then you get this warning. If you continue to do it then you get dismissed from school. If you continue to do it then you get suspended, and all those technical solutions. Elder Atum looked at me and said Nancy I

need you to slow. I need you just to slow down because the children are just the messengers and if we don't heal the community all those things you're doing over here are not going to change. And so we step back. I stepped off the edge and in pulled my staff back with me and said, guys we need to hang on. We need to work with The Cultural Wellness Center and help the community. (…) The biggest thing is the change in culture in the building you can walk through the building, and you can see students engaged in their learning that's hard to quantify but that's the real change and it's that change that's going to lead to high test scores.

At the time, the school was about 85 percent African American and 98 percent free and reduced lunch. The Culture Wellness program, created with Maxfield, made a huge impact on the students, in ways nothing else in the past had. They did this by working with the community to heal their wounds. Wounds created by generations of neglect and abuse form Minnesota's racist structure. Wounds like U.S. Census data showing that most Minnesota families of color now have median incomes about half those of their white neighbors.

The Culture Wellness Center made an impact on the Maxfield Magnet School by providing the school's community with education on physical, and mental wellness; African Identity; and by providing recourses for health, like food and winter clothes. Principle Stachel noted that "the set of resources that elder Atum brought to the table are not something that I (Principle Stachel) have available." I know this might not make much sense, but it will after I explain my reconstruction period with The Cultural Wellness Center.

Theory

Whenever we enter conversations about suffering and injustices, I think it's natural to come to one of two conclusions. One, you're consumed with an overwhelming feeling of hopelessness and sorrow. Or two, you respond to the struggle with a need to make a change. I think often, number one is the conclusion many meet when looking at unjust systems. The call to action, number two, is how many nonprofits and activist groups are born. In either situation, I want you to ask yourself; who's responsibility is it to make a positive change? Now ask yourself, whose responsibility is it to provide reparations to a community affected by structural racism and other oppressions? These are tricky questions. You might say change starts with those who have power and privilege [i.e.: governance and philanthropy]. Or that change starts with those who directly/indirectly benefit suffering communities. For this section of my research, I would like to introduce the asset-based approach to positive change in communities. Although this method is not a traditional route taken in community healing, I argue it is the most effective. Aid from outside organizations is like giving communities fish when they are hungry, while an asset-based approach is teaching the community to fish. An asset-based approach has potential to create long-term change and empowers a community for generations to come. The Cultural Wellness Center is an example of this kind change.

Assets based approaches are methods that create community development by facilitating people and communities to come together to achieve positive change using their knowledge, skills and lived experience of the issues they encounter in their own lives.

OUTSIDE AID=DEPENDENCY: In the article *Assets-based community development[1]* by John Kretzmann and John P. McKnight the authors stated, "The hard truth is that development must start from within the community and, in most of our urban neighborhoods, there is no other choice" (p. 23 – 29). There can only be true positive change if change comes from inside communities. Kretzmann and McKnight try to explain this through acknowledging the monolithic identities given to communities of color. The identity is synonymous with struggle and people in need of saving. This monolithic identity can create a self-concept within a community that they are consumers of services and can only be consumers of services. Kretzmann and McKnight state that, "Consumers of services focus vast amounts of creativity and intelligence on the survival-motivated challenge of outwitting the "system," or on finding ways - in the informal or even illegal economy - to bypass the system entirely." This identity creates little space for positive change.

Dependency solely grounded in the community; it's also present in outside organizations that provide aid. If the sole purpose of an organization is to support a struggling community, that community must always be in some sort of distress for organizations to continue to stay alive. This aid can end up perpetuating the community's suffering for the sake of helping the community. This unintended outcome can be avoided through an asset-based approach to healing.

ASSET-BASED APPROACH=INDEPENDENCE: It's important to say that Kretzmann and McKnight note that, focusing on the assets of lower income communities does not imply that these communities do not need additional resources from the outside. Rather, outside resources will be much more effectively used if the local community is itself fully mobilized and invested, and if it can define the agendas for which additional resources must be obtained. Asset-based approaches acknowledge that communities have the tools they need to create their positive change. At its root, asset-based approaches create change by the people for the people.

Asset-based approaches are an essential part of The Cultural Wellness Center's work. The center uses the tools of spiritual healing, symbolic and mythos understanding, and harmonium balance. These tools are found with ourselves. When these tools are utilized, they can achieve community/individual growth and healing. The center's focus is on guiding individual and groups in finding their spiritual, symbolic, mythos, and harmonium methods of thinking. When used together, these ways of thinking cultivate culture. Minkara Tezet, Griot of Psychology and Psychiatry at the center, described culture as, not a philosophy... cultural wellness is a way of living. It's a practice. I think as people become clearer about culture and what it can provide for you culture becomes a resource that you dip back into and say, 'oh, there's another way to think about the way you live. There's another way to think about how you take care of yourself.' And then when you become immersed in it, culture begins to teach you how to live.

The Cultural Wellness Center lives cultural wellness through the practices of cultural self-study, community leadership, intercultural interfacing, and in organizational culture. Cultural self-study is the practice of working with individuals to provide them with the knowledge and guidance that enhances their capacity and frame to do a cultural self-study. The self-study is a long-term process. A process that requires the commitment to research, writing, and being perfectly honest with oneself. Community Leadership is the process of discovering and developing leaders in their community. These leaders define what a healthy community looks like and develop ways to achieve that definition in their spaces. Intercultural interfacing is the shift from seeking everything through a racial lens to adopting a cultural frame of understanding. Organizations have their philosophies and ways of behaving in the world. Organizational culture is the process where leaders identify strategies for creating inclusive organizations to support their community.

The methods above were not invented by The Cultural Wellness Center. The center sees these tools as something that has always been in the individual and communities that they work with. Their work is highlighting these skills and abilities through practice and guidance. It's this method of leadership for social justice that makes The Cultural Wellness Center so unique in what they do. Tezet stated that culture doesn't fight structural racism; it fills a void that structural racism creates. Through identity, self-love, and self-understanding. Every person is born with, and into, culture. The Cultural Wellness Center taps into their innate skills to heal communities, and that is asset-based community development.

Action Plan

The work of The Cultural Wellness Center is beautiful. When I first learned of the center I was immediately drawn to their work. I am inspired by the center's ability to cultivate love, community, and healing within Minnesota's communities of color. The more that I learned about their methods of cultural wellness, the more I thought of ways that I can make a positive change in my community.

The Cultural Wellness Center's mission is to create lasting solutions for problems in their community. This mission is meant to fight structural racism in Minnesota. I grew up experiencing these impacts of structural racism, and I understand how important this work is. The Minnesota State Demographic Center reports that Minnesota is 81 percent white ("Age, Race, Ethnicity," 2015).[2] Furthermore, Jeff Wagner's online article states that Minnesota is also the second worse state when looking at racial disparities[3] ("Minnesota Ranked 2nd-Worst In U.S. For Racial Equality," 2017). As I already mentioned, these realities were evident to me while growing up in the state. This was especially clear to me while in school. Growing up I noticed that many of my peers of color didn't strive to excel inside or outside the classroom. Social conditioning and gaps in opportunity, education, and wealth often keep students of color from living prosperous, fulfilling lives. I've always been sensitive to this issue, and I would like to start a program that would inspire youth of color to aspire to be whomever they want to be. I've used three strategies of The Cultural Wellness Center to begin brainstorming ways to start this program.

Minnesota has a majority white education system. This means the education structure is built to support white students and students of color are often left behind. It should also be noted that MINNPOST reported that student of color and native students "make up nearly a third of the K-12 population ("Teachers of color reflect on navigating a mostly white education system," 2017). According to state data, out of the nearly 57,000 licensed teachers, only about 2,500 identified as Native American, Asian, Hispanic or black this past school year. In total, these teachers only account for four percent of the teacher corps ("Teachers of color reflect on navigating a mostly white education system," 2017)." Students are not seeing themselves represented their teachers. This also means that most teachers are disconnected from the social, economic, and educational barriers that students of colors face. I can personally say, as a person of color, that I watched as my peers felt left behind. If you think that that is a thing of the past, MPR wrote in a 2016 report, "the state's wide academic achievement gaps between white students and students of color also remain virtually unchanged, according to the scores." These scores came from the Minnesota Comprehensive Assessments, yearly tests in reading, math, and science.

The Culture Wellness Center has asset-based programs. The Center uses five strategies described by the social change wheel that I could apply to a program that helps students navigate these barriers. These strategies are education, grassroots organizing, community building, direct service, and political processes. Students of color are left behind in Minnesota education system. I would like to focus on students from middle school and follow them through high school.

Hopefully, a program like this can provide young students with the support they need to succeed.

EDUCATION: The first step would be to identify what barriers student of color face while in school. In an ideal world, this would include investigating the data school districts in Minnesota with a large proportion of students of color. After identifying these districts and the barriers they face, you can move onto the next step.

GRASSROOTS ORGANIZING: The next step would be to connect and collaborate with local grassroots organizations. It is important to find existing resources and allies that believe in your mission. Growing a network can help in implementing strategies and improving what already exists.

COMMUNITY BUILDING: This is the third and most important step. Students need role models that look like them. I can't stress how crucial this is. Social conditioning is a massive barrier for students to get over. When all that youth of color see in media, or in their lives, are stereotypes how will they know anything else? The Cultural Wellness Center has developed a model called Community Systems Navigators. The center says that in this model "community residents are trained by elders at our facility to become 'Navigators.' Navigators are matched to families with similar life experiences, and they help reconnect people to their culture and heritage to help build the self-efficacy necessary to transition from welfare to work ("OUR MODELS: *Community Systems Navigators*," 2017)." Community Systems Navigators would provide students with Elders and Navigators of color that can guide them in and outside of class. This does not always mean academically. It also means mentally, socially, and spiritually. Then students later become navigators themselves and spread what they have learned to other students of color. A support group with students of color who hold one another accountable would also sustain and grow this work.

DIRECT SERVICE: The fourth step would be creating activities which address immediate needs that students of color identify. Students will understand that they are seen, heard, understood, and cared for. The program and network of grassroots organizations could work together to provide for these needs for the student.

POLITICAL PROCESS: The last step would be creating activities that mobilize people to influence public policy through formal political channels: campaign work, voting, and voter registration. The unjust educational system comes from unjust policies that affect people of color. All the work done above is simply a Band-Aid on a larger structural issue that needs to be changed to sustain cultural wellness.

About the Author – Deborah Honore

I grew up in Twin Cities, Minnesota, but was born in Ethiopia. I am now a senior at the University of St. Thomas majoring in Justice & Peace Studies and Communication & Journalism. After graduation, I plan on working as a multimedia journalist reporting on environmental and social justice matters.

Works Cited

"Data by Topic: Age, Race & Ethnicity." *MN State Demographic Center*, 8 June 2017, mn.gov/admin/demography/data-by-topic/age-race-ethnicity/.

"Minnesota Ranked 2nd-Worst In the U.S. For Racial Equality." *WCCO | CBS Minnesota*, 22 Aug. 2017, minnesota.cbslocal.com/2017/08/22/minnesota-racial-inequality/.\08/14/17,

Erin Hinrichs |. "Teachers of Color Reflect on Navigating a White Education System." *MinnPost*, www.minnpost.com/education/2017/08/teachers-color-reflect-navigating-mostly-white-education-system.

Wastvedt, Solvejg. "New Data: Minn. Test Scores Stagnant, Achievement Gap Unchanged." *Minnesota Public Radio News*, 28 July 2016, www.mprnews.org/story/2016/07/28/minnesota-education-data-test-scores-stagnant-achievement-gap-remains.

"Our Models." *Cultural Wellness Center*, www.culturalwellnesscenter.org/about-us/models/.

Wastvedt, Solvejg. "New Data: Minn. Test Scores Stagnant, Achievement Gap Unchanged." *Minnesota Public Radio News*, 28 July 2016, www.mprnews.org/story/2016/07/28/minnesota-education-data-test-scores-stagnant-achievement-gap-remains.

Dream Refugee
Sunita Dharod

Story

The goal of refugees is to make it to a safe place. This is the shared opinion of many people who know about the refugee crisis, but what if the problem doesn't stop there? We would like to think it does, but refugees are faced quite harshly with a new set of problems barriers and challenges when they arrive to the place they've worked so hard to get to. The problem on our end is the lack of education we have about the refugee crisis and the lack of care shown to refugees starting their life in a completely new place. Whether it be in school, work or community environments, we must consider how environments may be challenging or unwelcoming to a refugee. The challenge refugees face can include culture shock, a language barrier, disconnect from community, lack of cultural needs such as specific groceries or a specific church.

Dream refugee brings the knowledge of the community. Since their board is from or familiar with the twin cities, they not only have connections, but feel confident in how to reach both the refugee and Minnesotan population. This required creator Mohamed Malim to build a board of experienced Individuals who would contribute to the base knowledge of Minnesota and its different communities. Today, this allows Dream refugee to work with refugee communities and actually be able to provide them with resources and answer their questions.

Dream refugee's story of self is rooted in its founder's story and his own and Mohamed has a very personal motivation for creating Dream refugee. This organizations leader follows his own story as he experienced major hardships at such as young age in a refugee camp in Dadaab, Kenya. He found basic necessitates to be out of reach… things that we take for granted such as running water and medical care. This story of suffering did not stop however when he came to America, and this is where the idea for dream refugee grew out of. The move to America came with a new set of challenges, including learning English, and creating a whole new life in America. These challenges are what dream refugee helps refugees with. The need for this work stems from Mohamed seeing what his parents created for him and mimicking that idea to become a model dream refugee follows. This specific story gives power to the idea that being a refugee does not end when one leaves the refugee camp. It is a part of that person, and they can carry challenges after they arrive to their new home.

Dream Refugees goal is to build community and support networks for refugees in their new communities. This is achieved using strategies that are close to the community, educational, and personal. For example, Dream refugee has put on events such as a panel of refugees. This was an opportunity for them to share their stories and give a community who may know little about refugees, a chance to learn now.

Their outcome continues to unfold, as they seek opportunities to grow their name. Dream refugee has started a mentorship program with refugee youth, as well as start to educate the University of St Thomas about refugees through programming. While these ideas develop, they are continuing with their refugee story project. This is accomplished by interviewing a refugee and taking their picture. Then the story is shared on Dream refugee's forms of social media which are

Facebook, Instagram, and Twitter, as well as on their website and in an emailed newsletter.

Theory

The danger of a single story is a concept explained in a TED talk by Chimamanda Ngozi Adichie that challenges our assumptions. This concept is when we consume literature or media about a specific group having certain characteristics or practices and generalize everyone who falls into that group as also having those characteristics and practices. This is problematic first because it does not allow us to see them as having other qualities than the ones we assume about them. Secondly, it also does not allow us to see what we may have in common with them. Third, these generalizations can be and usually are false as Adichie explains and are just extensions of stereotypes which can also be harmful.

One example of this is when Adichie visited Mexico. "There were endless stories of Mexicans as people who were fleecing the healthcare system, sneaking across the border, being arrested at the border" (TED) in the media before she went to Mexico she explained. When she actually went to Mexico however, she saw people going about their normal day. This shocked her at first, but then she experienced overwhelming shame as she realized she had been "so immersed in the media coverage of Mexicans that they had become one thing in [her] mind, the abject immigrant" (TED). She realized that she had bought into that single story of immigrants. This is how you create a single story she explains, "Show a group of people as one thing over and over again, and that is what they become" (TED).

Applying this to Dream Refugee, we can see that this organization intentionally shares refugee stories so that refugees do not fall into a single story. Since the only strict criteria for being featured on the website is being a refugee, the danger of having these stories become the same is avoided. In fact, the stories intentionally cover a variety of nationalities and experiences, refugees from across the globe. This is an example of leadership for social change because it creates a variety of stories for average Americans who may not have one story of refugees. The population that Dream refugee reaches and that need those stories are those who do not know about the refugee experience. Because of this, it would be easy for them to fall into having a single story of refugees. However, when they look into Dream Refugees stories, they are confronted with variety.

Currently Dream Refugee has eleven stories on their site, which is intentional in "showcase[ing] to the broader community the untold refugee experience [to] create empathy and compassion between disparate communities" (Stories). But empathy and compassion are large concepts to create. They are meaningful and take care to be able to evoke in someone. This is why the use of multiple stories is a tactic. It creates multiple opportunities for the reader to develop compassion and empathy.

"To insist on only these negative stories is to flatten my experience and to overlook the other stories that formed me. The single story creates stereotypes. And the problem with stereotypes is not that they are untrue, but that they are incomplete. They make one story become the only story" (TED). Looking at the refugee experience, we automatically have assumptions, a single story, or no story at all. However, if people are exposed to multiple refugee experiences and stories, stereotypes of refugees will be replaced with compassion and empathy for their different stories.

Action Planning

In order for an organization to effectively reach all types of people, solve different types of problems, and be as whole as they can, they must consider or implement all seven sections of the social change wheel. Dream refugee does a good job of implementing five out of the seven sections, which are as follows: charitable volunteerism, education, community building, grassroots organization, and confrontational strategies.

Dream refugee has established themselves as an organization that understands "charity and justice need not be mutually exclusive" (Klein). Which is how they build community. Through their mentorship program, they "help students who are or were refugees gain access to professional mentoring, scholarship aid, and a network

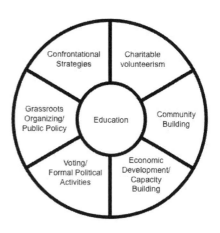

of connections in order to help them succeed in their high school and post-secondary education" (Home). They saw in this specific example, an intersection between serving refugee youth and building community with them at the same time. This is an example of both community building and charitable volunteering.

Surrounding the topic of education, Dream Refugee puts together various events for anyone in the community to go to and learn about the organization and the refugee experience. This past summer, they put together an event at the University of St. Thomas, where refugee and politician Ilhan Omar spoke about her experience to a group of community members and St. Thomas students, faculty and staff who attended.

In terms of confrontational strategies, the founder of Dream Refugee often speaks and meets people in person. This creates a confrontational person to person communication. This type of communication is important to establish trust and allows Dream Refugee to remain a humble organization. This is a confrontational strategy in their case because they often are starting these conversations in office hours and are persistent about following through.

In order to complete all points on the social change wheel, Dream Refugee must implement practices that reach voting/ formal political activities and economic development. Voting and formal political activities could be in the form of simply putting together a list of politicians who advocate for or who are making positive change for refugees, or who support foreign policy that favors refugees. This could be achieved through a tab on Dream Refugees website titled "political activism" or "how you can make a difference". In economic development, Dream Refugee could give back to schools as their core component is education. This could be in the form of money given to schools their mentee population attends. Funding could go directly to growing the communities in which refugee youth live.

Through these two actions, Dream Refugee can achieve both voting/ formal political activities and economic development, which would complete all points on the social change wheel and strengthen their work in support of refugees and their dreams. To get in contact, or follow Dream Refugee, visit their website at www.dreamrefugee.org

Works Cited

"Home." Dream Refugee, www.dreamrefugee.org/.

Klein, M. (2017). "Social change wheel analysis: Beyond the dichotomy of charity or justice," in Colon, C.; Gristwood, A. & Woolf, M. (2017). *Civil Rights and Inequalities, Occasional Publication #6*, Boston: CAPA, The Global Education Network.

"Stories." Dream Refugee, www.dreamrefugee.org/all-stories/.

TED talks Director. "The Danger of a Single Story | Chimamanda Ngozi Adichie." YouTube, 7 Oct. 2009, www.youtube.com/watch?v=D9Ihs241zeg.

About the Author – Sunita Dharod

I am a junior studying justice and peace and American culture and difference at St. Thomas. I have passions for animal rights, photography, music, and racial justice, which I am always trying to apply and intersect.

I have multiple leadership positions on campus, which is why I think reflecting on what it means to be a leader is important. I have grown through amazing leaders in my life that I have met from programs like VISION; a global community building trip opportunity that I have been a part of since freshman year. The leaders I had on my first trip really taught me the value of being a humble and down to earth leader in their care for all of us participants. I have also learned from people like my high school videography teacher, Mr. Fornicoia that showing your passion for your art and work is beneficial to those with whom you work.

Finnegan's Beer
Raquel Sternitzke

"Childhood hunger is a solvable problem. We have enough food. We have programs in place to reach kids. What's needed is to remove the barriers that keep kids from accessing those programs". – Billy Shore

Story

The CEO and founder of Finnegan's, Jacquie Berglund, found her calling in entrepreneurship while she was living in France, training government officials about the market economy (Finnegan's). Berglund completed her undergraduate degree in communications and political science at Augsburg College and received a Masters of Arts Degree in International Relations and Diplomacy from the American Graduate School in Paris, France. Through her work in France she realized that change was happening as the grassroots level, so she wanted to create a business that could engage the local community. Berglund moved back to Minnesota in 1997, and while Berglund was thinking about which social issues she wanted to address, she attended a talk given by hunger advocate Billy Shore and was moved to get involved in eradicating hunger in her local area. In 2000 Berglund launched Finnegan's.

They are working to eradicate hunger in an innovative way by selling beer to private vendors for distribution, funneling 100% of their profits into their charity fund, and then donating the money in the fund to local food shelves for them to buy fresh produce from local growers to stock their shelves (Finnegan's). They are the first beer company in the world to give 100% of their profits to charity, and they are the second longest running social enterprise to donate 100% of their profits. It took nine years for the company to gain popularity, with issues such as low profitability and a divorce from her husband in the middle of the formative time, but the hard work that Berglund put in, along with the support from Summit Brewing Company, four full-time staff members, one part-time staff member, and many volunteers, eventually paid off. Finnegan's is currently the tenth largest Minnesota beer company. In 2016 Finnegan's raised $1,033,000 through donations and profits. Finnegan's donates to 5 food shelves throughout the Midwest: Great Plains Food Bank in North Dakota, Feeding South Dakota, Foodbank of Iowa, The Food Group in Minnesota, and Hunger Task Force in Wisconsin.

Theory

The traditional path of dealing with social justice issues is one that focuses on "a community's needs, deficiencies and problems" (Kretzmann, J., & McKnight, J. P., 1996, p 23) and tends to do less to integrate into affected communities and instead sets up systems of aid that offers services with the hope of combating injustice. The assets-based community development finds its strength by giving decision-making power to those within the affected community and attempts to map out "gifts, skills and capacities on the community's residents" (Kretzmann, J., & McKnight, J. P., 1996, p 27). While John Kretzmann and John P. McKinght, who wrote the article I am using as reference on assets-based community development, make a case that is clearly in favor of the assets-based approach, I am less concerned with picking which path is better and more interested in using their theory in order to consider how the structure of power in Finnegan's fits into their theory and I hope that in doing so I will find inspiration for an action step for Finnegan's.

The traditional path to taking on social issues within a community tends to be needs driven and considers what issues need to be addressed within communities and what is the most efficient path to immediate and effective help. In many ways Finnegan's works within the traditional path. The founder of Finnegan's recognized the issue of hunger in her community, felt compelled to get involved by using her entrepreneurial knowledge, and created an innovative organization that is giving over a million dollars a year to a local food shelves so that fresh produce from local farms can be stocked. The organizational system of Finnegan's is one that raises a lot of money, gets people thinking about their buying power, and has been very successful, but it is not a democratic system and it doesn't put the majority of its decision-making into the hands of the communities they are trying to help. Finnegan's has a vertical power structure that works for its organization because its work is focused mostly on fundraising for food shelves. Because Finnegan's is essentially a fundraising tool, it is important to consider how the food shelves they donate too, such as The Food Group in Minnesota, as well as other organizations that partner with Finnegan's, structure their organizational leadership.

The Food Group also has a vertical structure of leadership that is expected for an organization of its size. The Food Group has many different programs relating to hunger and poverty, but the one that I found that involves local communities the most is their work on sustainable agriculture with the MN Food Association. According to The Food Group's website, "Through operation of certified organic farm land we offer land-based farmer education for immigrant and minority farmers, youth and community farm programming, urban ag development, and an annual farmer education conference" (The Food Group). This initiative works directly with people living in communities and gives some power to people, but it is not as integrating as an assets-based approach.

In addition to the work that Finnegan's does with The Food Group, it also uses its popularity and resources to work in conjunction with other local organizations, such as Start Reading Now. In order to engage with Finnegan's Beer, I went to a Drink Like You Care (DLYC) event that Finnegan's partnered with Start Reading Now in order to fundraise for the organization at a local bar. Start Reading Now, which holds book fairs for children in low-income families, joined with Finnegan's so that 100% of the profits made from Finnegan's beer that night would go towards supporting the organization. When Finnegan's works with local organizations they are giving the power to organizations to work with the money made and it seems to be a type of an assets-based approach. Finnegan's recognizes the power of other organizations and allows them to profit from Finnegan's fundraising and use the money for their work in bettering the community.

Action Planning

When considering the Social Change Wheel, Finnegan's practices direct service in their approach to social justice. Other aspects of the Social Change Wheel are practiced by nonprofit organizations they support and raise money for, but Finnegan's itself focuses largely on direct service in their work with food shelves. I believe that Finnegan's can draw  from other aspects of the Social Change Wheel in order to enhance the impact of the justice work they're doing. Considering the assets-based approach, community building is an aspect of the Social Change Wheel that could be adopted by Finnegan's that would hopefully engage with other parts of the Social Change Wheel, such as education and capacity building.

Due to the nature of Finnegan's' work, it is not feasible for them to adopt a completely assets-based approach or a democratic style of leadership. However, I propose the creation of community gardens in areas affected by hunger as a step towards integrating with the community they are serving. The creation of a community garden, which should be maintained by people within the community, would be a great way to use the assets of the community. Community gardens allow for leadership positions to be held, engagement with fellow members of the community to be experienced, a skill set to be taught, and fresh produce to be available to those experiencing hunger. Buying land to be used for community gardens, promoting the garden in order to get community members involved, and donating seeds and tools needed for garden would be a great way for Finnegan's to integrate better with the communities they serve.

In order for Finnegan's beer to create the community garden, they will need to take steps in order to get the project running. The very first step to creating a community garden is to form a planning committee. In this first step Finnegan's can use an assets-based approach to identify community leaders and community members who would be beneficial to the creation of the garden, and to give them the space to beginning discussion and planning about the garden. Ideally the planning committee will adopt a democratic system of leadership and they will divvy up tasks between members. Some of the tasks taken on will include finding the right land to plant a garden (considering lighting, soil, and availability of water), deciding on system of how to spend budget, community outreach for work crew volunteers, develop garden design, and conditions for membership (American Community Garden Association).

At the core of Finnegan's Beer, they want to eradicate hunger. Hunger and poverty go hand in hand with the widespread inequality and structural oppression that many living in the U.S. face today. It is important for direct service, such a food shelf, to work to feed those who are in immediate need. But if we, as a society, are going to make a long-term impact on hunger, we need to consider the reasons why people face hunger and poverty and implement plans in order to better the lives of people in a long-lasting way. My hope is that a community garden can act as the first step towards community building, education, and capacity building so that structural injustice can turn into a shared strive towards justice.

Works Cited

American Community Garden Association. (n.d.). Tips on Starting a Community Garden. Retrieved December 21, 2017, from https://aggie-horticulture.tamu.edu/kindergarden/CHILD/COM/COMMUN.HTM

Finnegan's . (n.d.). Jacquie Berglund Bio. Retrieved December 18, 2017, from http://Finnegan's.org/jacquie-berglunds-bio/

Finnegan's . (n.d.). Community Fund. Retrieved December 18, 2017, from https://Finnegan's.org/community-fund-about/

Kretzmann, J., & McKnight, J. P. (1996). Assets-based community development. National Civic Review, 85.4, p 23, p 27. Retrieved November 20, 2017.

The Food Group. (n.d.). Our Programs. Retrieved November 21, 2017, from https://thefoodgroupmn.org/about-us/programs/

About the Author – Raquel Sternitzke

From an education in the intersection of Justice and Peace Studies and Comparative Theology and Interreligious Studies, I study the role of religion in creating and continuing systems of injustice and conflict, as well as the role religion plays in advocating for social justice and mediating conflict, so that people, living in a world of diverse religions and complex social issues, can coexist peacefully and justly by understanding the complexities of social, theological, cultural and political aspects of religion and considering how each aspect shapes the worldview of religious practitioners.

Green Garden Bakery
Anita Dharod

"Without a sense of caring, there can be no sense of community."
—Anthony D'Angelo

Story

The kids of Heritage Park in Minneapolis, Minnesota faced a problem. They lived in a food desert- a place lacking access to fresh fruit, vegetables, and other whole foods. This means, that within a 10-mile radius, there were no stores offering healthy foods. In most suburbs of Minnesota, you can find multiple big-chain grocery stores within 5 miles of a community, but Heritage Park community members would have to shop at convenience stores or gas stations to buy groceries. Many people took the bus in order to go to a better grocery store that offered healthy food. The Heritage Park community is under-served compared to wealthier areas of Minnesota, and they want to change that.

The non-profit Urban Strategies had been coming to Heritage Park since 2010, teaching community members how to cook delicious and healthy foods. They taught kids how to make smoothies, deserts, salads and how to exercise their imagination to create new recipes. They also started a community garden that they could harvest from for their cooking classes. Alfonso Williams, one of the founders of Green

Garden talked about how Urban Strategies played a role in GG. He said, "One day me and some friends were walking back from school and we smelled something really great. We went to see what it was and we saw the Urban Strategies cooking class at work" -so he and a few of his friends decided to sign up for cooking classes (A. Williams, personal interview, October 7, 2017). This was the beginning of Green Garden Bakery.

In the class, while kids learned how to make healthy foods using veggies they collected from a community garden, they had an idea. They knew that their community was a food desert. They knew that they had the skills to change their own community. The goal was to address the ways they had been overlooked through their own business. They wanted to start their own sustainable bakery selling the food that they had learned how to make. Food that would be healthy, sustainable, sold at a fair price while also providing fair-paying jobs to youth.

They invested in perfecting their recipes, starting with tomato cakes. Tomato cakes were made with green tomatoes that were harvested from the garden the previous season. They started preparing for their first opportunity to show their product at the Global Market Green Fair in 2014. As they were preparing for this, their close friend Amarya was in a car accident. She had been paralyzed from the waist down. Although their friend was not one of the founding members of Green Garden, she had grown up with the group who had founded it and was supportive of their business. She was scheduled to be enrolled in the Urban Strategies cooking class before her accident. The Green Garden Bakery team decided to use 1/3 of the profits they made to donate to their friend's medical bills. Now there was extra pressure for Green Garden to succeed.

As the day for the Global Market Green Fair approached, the Garden Bakery had the perfect tomato cake recipe and they were confident and prepared to show their creation. Their stand at the fair ended up gaining over 1000 dollars in profit- better than the team had expected. It was a success!

After their venture into the Global Green Market Fair, the team decided they really could turn their dream into a reality and make Green Garden a community business. They started working with Urban Strategies to perfect more recipes. Now the bakery has 5 different items on their menu: Beet Brownie Bites, Carrot Pumpkin Bread, Green Tomato Cakes, Lemon Zucchini Muffins, and Jalapeño Chocolate Chip Cookies. Selling their baked goods to community members at a pay-what-you-can price ensured that no matter what your economic status was, you could enjoy healthy food. They have expanded their community garden to keep up with the rising amount of orders they get. They have partnered with Whole Foods and are able to set up a stand at their store to sell their sustainable, healthy food at a fixed price. They have also started catering to community meetings and other events.

Although the main goal of Green Garden Bakery was to help make healthy food available in the Heritage Park food desert- the kids have accomplished much more. They have raised money for 12 community fundraisers including a Voice-to-Text translation program for their friend Amarya who was paralyzed, groceries for families, exercise classes, and security systems for four families who were robbed. They have also created a business that will continually benefit their community. The Green Garden Bakery plans to always be youth led. Once the current leaders of the bakery move off to college or graduate, other youth leaders in the community will take their place. The garden will continue to be a resource for those in the community who want healthy food. The Green Garden Bakery leaders say that their long term goal is to open up a store front for Green Garden in the neighborhood. They are working on funding this and hopefully we will see a Green Garden Bakery in Heritage Park in a few years.

Theory

All too often, under-served communities targeted by "needs-based" organizations that turn them into "clients", relying on the resources of outsiders to fill their needs (Kretzmann and McKnight,

1996, p. 24). There are many problems with this. It leads community members to think that they are unable to survive without this help. Instead of feeling empowered, these people are targeted for their "problems, needs and deficiencies" (Kretzmann and McKnight, 1996, p. 23). A better approach that can be used to serve low-income neighborhoods, according to Kretzmann and McKnight (1996), is an *assets-based* approach. Instead of focusing on the problems, needs, and deficiencies of a neighborhood, we should focus on assets. In this approach a community evaluates what assets it has in its individuals, associations, and institutions and uses these for the greater good of the neighborhood. After this, a community can more confidently *ask* organizations for what resources they need instead of being *told* what they need. Heritage Park is a community that effectively used an assets-based approach by finding talents in their own community to start Green Garden Bakery, and then partnering with the non-profit Urban Strategies to gain access to even more resources that Green Garden Bakery could use.

Green Garden Bakery is asset-based, internally focused, and relationship driven- the three pillars of the Alternative Community Development Path. Green Garden Bakery is a business that took what was present in their community, the cooking skills of kids in Heritage Park, desire for healthy food in the neighborhood, and natural leaders that were already in the community before Green Garden started. They used those assets - the things they were most talented at- to create a business.

Green Garden can be defined as internally focused. Kretzmann and McKnight believe that internally-focused community development is more likely to succeed because community members are more actively interested in improving their own communities rather than passively watching an outside organization fix things. Green Garden Bakery is a business that is very invested in their own community. Leaders and employees at GGB are all members of the community: most go to high school together. Instead of trying to make a large profit by selling to communities outside Heritage Park that might be able to pay more, GGB makes sure that they sell most of their baked goods back to the community for a 'pay-what-you-can' price. They form a relationship with the local grocers in the community to sell their product at stores that might not otherwise be able to offer healthy foods because of the cost. So, they make sure that they are focusing on the needs of their community at all times, and in doing so, they have created a support system with their high school, developed customers within Heritage Park, and formed partnerships grocery store owners.

Finally, Green Garden Bakery is relationship driven. Kretzmann and McKnight say that the idea that "people can count on their neighbors and neighborhood resources…has weakened" which is unfortunate because relationship building is instrumental in a community's success (Kretzmann and McKnight, 1996, p. 23). Green Garden Bakery's leaders have recognized the importance of maintaining relationships. First, they have a relationship with the non-profit Urban Strategies. Urban Strategies first started teaching cooking classes to the local high school. GGB approached them with their business idea and they agreed to support the business. They have a relationship with local community businesses and grocers who agree to let Green Garden Bakery sell their food in front of their stores. Finally, they have a great relationship with their community. The community supports GGB by buying their food, and GGB supports the community by donating 1/3 of their profits to community activities and fundraisers.

Green Garden Bakery's business model shows how a community that works together and focuses on strengths can succeed.

Action Planning

As Green Garden Bakery continues to grow, they will face new challenges. They have already anticipated these challenges, and plan to open up a store front as a solution. The SWOT analysis is a tool used to asses to strengths, weaknesses, opportunities, and threats Green Garden Bakery faces. By using the SWOT analysis, Green Garden

Bakery can have a better idea of why they need a storefront, and what resources they can tap into to get funding for their store.

Every business has its own unique set of strengths and weaknesses. Green Garden Bakery is no different. They have a team that works together very well- a group of high school students who share a common goal of serving their community healthy food. The employees all have a willingness and excitement to learn. Another strength they have is that their product is different from others in the market- it can be hard to find vegan, gluten free, sustainably- produced foods and GGB caters to people who want this kind of food. They have strong connections with the nation-wide non-profit Urban Strategies, the after school program at their high school, and community members who buy their food. Finally, they have experience presenting their business- they have a speech they pitch to possible sponsors, business awards committees, and reporters. They currently have 30 sponsors including Whole Foods, Clif Bar, and the University of Minnesota.

Green Garden has some weaknesses. First, because it was founded and is now run by high school students, they don't have the same background as most business owners. Most business owners are a bit older and have a considerable amount of experience in business before they decide to open up their own store- some even have college degrees in business. In contrast, GGB is a first job for many of its leaders- despite the steep learning curve, they have proven themselves to be successful and capable business owners. Another weakness is that a few student leaders have a 4-year max period that they will be working at GGB, because that's how long they are in high school. Some of the youth leaders say they plan to still be involved while they are in college, but they won't be able to commit the same amount of time as they do now. This means that the team that works together so well now might not be the same team in four years.

The external points in the SWOT analysis- their opportunities and threats can be used to plan a strategy for GG. Green Garden has a lot of opportunities in Minnesota. There are several businesses that are interested in sustainability that Green Garden could partner with (ex. Brightside, Whole Foods, J. Selby's). Green Garden can apply for grants in Minnesota- recently they received a grant from the General Mills North Minneapolis Food System Grant Program (Emond, 2017). Some threats to Green Garden are well established brands selling similar products to them. Another threat is the unpredictability of the crops GGB relies on from their community garden- bad weather or other factors may mean GGB doesn't have any ingredients to work with. Finally, Green Garden currently relies on bigger businesses to help them with space they don't have. For example, another company lets GGB rent out a space in their facilities to store their food in the winter. If any of these companies were to shut down or decide they didn't have space for GGB, they would have a problem.

The SWOT analysis leads to the idea of a storefront as a conclusion. The internal points of SWOT helps us see if the idea of a storefront would work. Because GGB has a great presence and strong relationships within the community, they have enough support to bring a storefront to Heritage Park. Their experience presenting to possible donors means they are capable of getting funding from outside organizations. Their weaknesses are unlikely to prevent them from opening a storefront. The external points of SWOT helps us see how they will work outside of their community to make their dream a reality. One of the threats to their business was that GGB didn't have their own storage facility- a storefront would solve that. Another threat was that GGB wasn't as established as other brands- a storefront would help them gain visibility and become more established in Minnesota. Finally, GGB has opportunities to use their current donors, the non-profit Urban Strategies, and other community members identified in the 'strengths' portion to help them gain access to new donors.

If you are inspired by Green Garden Bakery's work, their amazing team, or their creative leadership style, take a look at their website (greengardenbakery.weebly.com). You can place an order online for catering and try some of their delicious food, donate supplies or ingredients by checking out their Amazon wish list, or volunteer with them!

Works Cited

Emond, Stacy. (2017 April 6). Increasing Healthy Food Access in Northern Minneapolis. *Greater Twin Cities United Way.* https://www.gtcuw.org/increasing-healthy-food-access-north-minneapolis.

John Kretzmann and John P. McKnight. (1996). Asset Based Community Development. *National Civic Review.* 85.4.

Who We Are. Green Garden Bakery. Web. http://greengardenbakery.weebly.com

About the Author – Anita Dharod

I am currently a student at the University of St. Thomas, majoring in public relations. I am passionate about food justice, animal rights, and cultural diversity.

I have learned about leadership from my parents who taught me to be confident in making decisions and standing up for what I believe in, from my high school videographer teacher Nick Fornicoia who taught me that good leaders encourage mistakes and learning, and from my rowing coach Sarah Monn who taught me the importance of patience and teambuilding.

This year, I had the opportunity to learn more about leadership from the Green Garden Bakery team, my professor Mike Klein, and students in my Leadership for Social Justice class.

Habitat for Humanity-Twin Cities
Andrew H. Morgenstern

Housing is absolutely essential to human flourishing. Without stable shelter, it all falls apart.
- Matthew Desmond, American sociologist

Story

     Although everyone experiences childhood, it is sometimes the most underrated time of a person's life. Childhood is the time when foundations are laid for the life that a person will live. It is the time when individuals discover their talents and gifts, a time when they can learn and experiment with little obligation, and a time when they can be free to experience the world with all its beauties. Every person's childhood is a gem that shapes them into the person that he or she will become in the future. Most first world citizens take all of this for granted, but the rest of the world often isn't as fortunate. Even in the first world, the average middle-class American child builds a personal foundation with little interference from negative outside factors, while children of lower-class families are often split between experiencing childhood and maintaining life stability. This is a reality for roughly one in every three Americans children simply because their families face housing challenges (Ingraham, 2014). This is a reality that Yemane and Bizunesh didn't want their children to have to suffer. "The home is everything" according to an old Ethiopian proverb (Hagerman, 2016). It is the place to live and to learn. The place where there is freedom to have pain and hunger as well as joy and love. It is the place that provides shelter and protection and emboldens its residents to challenge themselves and take risks.

Yemane and Bizunesh moved to the United States from Ethiopia in 2012. They brought with them two daughters, Miracle and Kenaket, and two sons, Gemachis and Amanuel. Yemane was a history teacher in Ethiopia prior to having children and had firsthand experience witnessing the results of political and military conflict. He also understood the basic workings of Abraham Maslow's theory on the hierarchy of human needs (Maslow, 1943). For a person to get to the point where they can pursue and experience self-actualization they must first fulfill the four levels of needs below it. A community where political and military conflict regularly occur creates an environment where housing becomes unstable. Unstable housing undermines the first and second needs in Maslow's theory, shelter and the safety of property, and destroys any chance at living a life in which individuals can realize their full potential.

When Yemane and his wife moved to the United States, they hoped to escape their toxic environment. Unfortunately, they, like many non-European immigrants, experienced economic troubles in the US. Their first home, a duplex in Minneapolis, was nothing like what they wanted their children to grow up in. It embodied everything they had wanted to avoid in moving away from Ethiopia – it was overcrowded, busy, and dangerous. This initially discouraged Yemane and Bizunesh. They felt misled regarding the ideals and prosperity that the Land of the Free had to offer, but they were determined to create a place where their children could experience self-actualization.

After searching for a better way forward, Yemane and Bizunesh learned of the work of Habitat for Humanity Twin Cities. On the surface, it appeared to be a community service organization that championed the idea of providing affordable houses to families in need. They determined that putting in an application for purchasing a house would be worthwhile. The process seemed strange at first since, as potential future homeowners, they were required to go to classes on financial literacy and basic household management and upkeep. Also, part of the process was the requirement that they take part in the construction of their future home. More than once they questioned why they needed to be so involved in the process. It didn't seem to be very efficient to have them, people with little construction experience, slowing down the building of the home.

One afternoon when their home was half complete, Yemane and Bizunesh were putting up drywall in their future basement to when they were struck with an epiphany. Just a couple of months before, they had made no investment with Habitat for Humanity Twin Cities. During the time since then they had moved from a perspective of simply wanting a safe home for their children to grow up in to actively doing something about it. And not only were they just doing something, they were creating a home to which they would feel connected. And this was happening through a process in which they had learned so much. This would be a home that would help build in them a pride in their own actions. This was the answer to the question that had been constantly nagging them through the entire process. Habitat for Humanity Twin Cities wasn't just a community service organization that builds affordable houses for people. Habitat for Humanity Twin Cities is an organization that uses community service to help families build homes for themselves. Through their labor Yemane and Bizunesh were establishing true ownership of their home. Their efforts would drive them to respect what they created and be thankful for the opportunity that they have been given. Such gratitude would lead to further service and a desire to give back to the community that has been generous to them.

Today Yemane and Bizunesh live in their home in West St. Paul with their four children. In their free-time they serve the community that they are so proud to be a part of and help other Habitat for Humanity Twin Cities future homeowners to understand the part they play in the process. They enjoy seeing their children play, go to school, ask questions, goof around, experiment, and do all the other things children do to better understand their world. And today this takes place in a home where they do not have to worry about whether their children have the stability that they need.

Theory

Today, urban centers have been associated with two extremes on the economic spectrum. On one side, there are the prospering economic elite who find their place at corporate America's massive business holdings within major cities. On the other hand, there are the people of low socio-economic status who inhabit the streets and overcrowded apartments of the inner cities. Some may say that these extremes create a needed balance, but most will argue that there is a problem that needs to be addressed. Rather than criticizing upper class society to shrink the gap between the two groups, many people from outside the community in need have taken it upon themselves to help the lower class. They have devoted many hours of service, fundraising, and advocacy while attempting to bring about lasting change within the communities. All too often this is the only route that is taken in an attempt to create change. People are then surprised when communities, where countless hours have been invested into change-making, continue to be dysfunctional. John Kretzmann and John McKnight refer to this as the traditional path, or a needs-driven strategy, which "can only guarantee survival, and can never lead to serious change or community development" (Kretzmann and McKnight, 1996). When only needs-driven strategy is implemented in a community, there is a high likelihood that the sense of hopelessness will be strengthened; where it seems that the likelihood of genuine change is zero.

In contrast to the "dead end" that comes from the needs-driven strategy, Kretzmann and McKnight propose a second strategy that can have lasting impact on a community. He calls this asset-based community development (Kretzmann and McKnight, 1996). The asset-based approach to community development is one that relies on the "assets" that a community can bring to the table. This approach allows for community members to use the resources and skills that they already possess to shape their own community. While the needs-driven strategy is based on a system of regular intervention by outside people and resources, the asset-based model focuses on limiting the amount of outside decision-making so as to enable change that can be owned and continued by the community. Habitat for Humanity has had a long history of community involvement and has taken up an asset-based approach to community development. This is evident through the works of the Habitat for Humanity-Twin Cities' Neighborhood Revitalization Program which has put much of its attention on empowering and enabling people to take ownership of their own communities.

Habitat for Humanity-Twin Cities, or H4H-TC for short, has sold more than 1,100 homes to families since 1985 (Humanity). These homes have been built in neighborhoods throughout the Twin Cities metro. These neighborhoods may be, but are not always, going through tough times as a community. Two examples are the Frogtown Neighborhood in Saint Paul and Jordan Neighborhood in North Minneapolis, both which are communities where H4H-TC has built homes. These communities both struggle with high unemployment, high crime-rates, and low income. While building homes provides families with a means of stability, H4H-TC has also recognized that more than home construction can be done to help communities in need. In 2011, H4H-TC began its Neighborhood Revitalization Program. The goal of the program is to work closely with local communities to empower members to take control of creating impactful change for their neighborhood while fostering an environment for others to get involved. The primary method for pursuing this goal has been through bringing communities together in a social or business setting to speak about issues of concern to community members, then providing inputs that enables those same community members to implement change.

Polina Montes de Oca, the current manager of the Neighborhood Revitalization Program, shares that H4H-TC is currently working with both the Frogtown and Jordan neighborhoods to create meaningful change by bringing community members together. The asset-based community development model is implemented in working with each of the two communities. Since each community is unique, so are the strategies used by H4H-TC to connect with each neighborhood. In the case of the Frogtown Neighborhood, the residents are hesitant for change in community dynamics because of uncertainty of where such changes will lead but show interest in incremental steps towards improving the community. Because of this H4H-TC has invested much time in building trust with the community members and empowers individuals within the community to lead events and bring the community together. This ensures that any change that is made doesn't seem forced and will be implemented with the approval of a majority of the community and at a pace that won't catch anyone off guard. In the Jordan Neighborhood there is an already established neighborhood association. This association is willing to collaborate with H4H-TC and is all in for change and breaking stigmas. This method of approaching change through the confrontational breaking of stigmas and quick movement towards change in the community is different, not better or worse, than that of the Frogtown Neighborhood as it relies on an intermediary party to instigate change.

The asset-based approach to community development, when utilized correctly, can create change that is both meaningful and impactful. In the case of H4H-TC work with the Neighborhood Revitalization Program, the asset-based approach to community development is being used to allow communities in the Twin Cities, which historically have struggled, to seek out improvement and to better the lives of the individuals living in these neighborhoods. As the Neighborhood Revitalization Program continues to espouse this perspective of creating change while expanding to other neighborhoods, there may be a point in time when the program becomes obsolete. A time may come when neighborhoods begin reaching out to one another to improve the broader community. At that point, an outside organization like H4H-TC prompting community organizing would be redundant and would not be needed other than as an advisory resource. If everything goes as desired, the Neighborhood Revitalization Program may just work itself out of existence in the Twin Cities.

Action Plan

The title of this book implies to all who read it that everything within represents social justice at its finest. But what really is social justice? Social justice is a relatively abstract concept to most people. In our world today, there are people who like to chalk up nearly any act of kindness as a work of social justice. And on the other side of the spectrum there are people who see social justice as something pursued by only one of the two major political parties and gets epitomized as being needed by only a few social groups. In contrast to both of these perspectives, social justice is differentiated from acts of service by the type of work that is done and the implications that come with it. Social justice should not be dictated by any political or social agenda. Social justice is about creating a world where all individuals experience freedom, equality, and opportunity.

The following section makes the argument that Habitat for Humanity-Twin Cities (H4H-TC) is an organization that embodies leadership for social justice through its collective action. The collective actions of H4H-TC will be presented using the social change wheel which illustrates multiple strategies that organizations use towards creating justice. Every organization working for social justice is unique and because of that each implements its own combination of different strategies. In the case of H4H-TC, the four strategies that it utilizes are community building, education, capacity building, and direct service.

Community building, alluded to earlier in the works of the Neighborhood Revitalization Program, is an element of the work of

H4H-TC that has value for the greater Minnesota and Midwest community as well as the Twin Cities. Helping develop leaders - in communities such as the Frogtown and Jordan neighborhoods - to organize around a certain problem and bond as a community creates space for people to be given a voice. When people are given a voice, change is bound to occur on a social level that they care for the most. Such change, while it may be relatively small, can make all the difference toward creating a community where people feel safe and empowered. Currently, the Frogtown and Jordan neighborhoods are two of the most troubled communities in the Twin Cities, but if they were to become empowered and feel safe then there is nothing to say that the rest of the Twin Cities couldn't follow suit. If the Twin Cities were to come together then so could the rest of the state. The implications of the concept of community development have no limits as to the scale that can be reached while beginning from the lowest level. Social justice is about creating freedom, equality, and opportunity. When starting from the lowest level and moving up, all three of these objectives can be achieved.

The other three strategies that H4H-TC implements for social justice are education, capacity building, and direct service. These strategies work together to form Habitat for Humanity's foundation. Habitat for Humanity began as the brain child of Clarence Jordan and Millard and Linda Fuller. The concept came from the idea of "partnership housing" on the Koinonia Farm, a community farm that allowed for those in need of shelter to work side by side with volunteers to create decent, affordable housing (Habitat's history). Partnership housing brought with it opportunities for education and capacity building in addition to the direct service that was occurring.

Education is key to creating social justice as it not only gives people the ability to understand the world around them but also enables people to research and develop means by which they can create for themselves meaningful change for the social justice. Education directly combats ignorance. Ignorance keeps people in the dark and whilst in the dark these people stumble about not knowing what direction they are headed. Ignorance is one the primary boundaries to equality and opportunity since equality is gauged by understanding where one is currently and the opportunities that exist for movement in the direction desired. Research and developing means for creating change emphasize freedom as they enable individuals to seek out methods for creating change that is meaningful to them. Individuals who can make decisions towards creating change embody the freedom that they have to do so.

Capacity building brings about social justice in its own unique ways. In the case of H4H-TC, future homeowners are given financial coaching, budgeting training, and mortgage foreclosure classes. Each of these contribute to a homeowner's feeling of economic safety and housing stability. While such safety and stability are in place, families do not have to worry about watching their backs all the time and will be of a sounder mind. This enables individuals to direct attention and energy towards functioning within a socially just system. Just as Maslow's Hierarchy of Needs, people are not able to pursue self-actualization until the lower, more basic needs are met (Maslow, 1943). Safety and stability are two of those needs that are met by capacity building.

Direct service is the last of the three strategies that contribute to H4H-TC's establishment of an environment of social justice. While direct service is not always a means for establishing social justice, when paired with capacity building and education it becomes a helpful element that an organization may utilize. Service is a way that an organization can directly influence the situations of those in need. For H4H-TC this means providing people with decent and affordable housing and ensuring that families have the proper physical tools and resources to keep up their new homes. By utilizing volunteers in the building process, H4H-TC involves individuals from outside of the community where the home is being built to help with the actual construction. This creates not only an awareness of housing issues but also connects outsiders to the community in which the homes are being built. Such connections create relationships that may be essential to communities working with and helping each other in the future. By bringing communities together, social justice will be realized as freedom, equality, and opportunity will be shared amongst the communities' members.

Habitat for Humanity-Twin Cities is a fine example of an organization whose mission is focused on creating social justice. Currently social justice is being realized through the collective actions of community building, education, capacity building, and direct service. By focusing on these strategies and perfecting how they are implemented, H4H-TC creates a space for many individuals to exercise their freedom, equality, and opportunity. With this comes positive change which combines with the work of many other justice-minded organizations in moving the world towards being more socially just.

Works Cited

Habitat's history. (n.d.). Retrieved December 12, 2017, from https://www.habitat.org/about/history

Hagerman, J. (2016, September 14). "Yaa Mana Ofii" -- Home is Everything for Habitat Homebuyers. Retrieved December 18, 2017, from https://www.tchabitat.org/blog/yaa-mana-ofii-home-is-everything-for-habitat homebuyers

Humanity, T. C. (n.d.). About Twin Cities Habitat. Retrieved November 26, 2017, from https://www.tchabitat.org/about

Ingraham, C. (2014, October 29). Child poverty in the U.S. is among the worst in the developed world. Retrieved December 18, 2017, from https://www.washingtonpost.com/news/wonk/wp/2014/10/29/child-poverty-in the-u-s-is-among-the-worst-in-the-developed-world/?utm_term=.f2b5b8b17fff

Kretzmann, J., & McKnight, J. P. (1996). Asset-Based Community Development. National Civic Review, 85(4), 23. Retrieved November 15, 2027, from http://go.galegroup.com/ps/i.do?p=EAIM&sw=w&u=clic_stthomas&v=2.1&id=GALE7CA19212826&it=r&asid=a69fb7307bf9b6159b01ac6b45deceb9.

Maslow, A. H. (1943). A Theory of Human Motivation. Psychological Review, 50(4), 370-96.

About the Author – Andrew H. Morgenstern

I am a third-year student at the University of St Thomas, currently studying mechanical engineering. I come from a lower middle-class family that has spent a large period of time working internationally in Russia and Ukraine as missionaries, where we worked with and reached out to low and middle-class people who struggled to sustain their material and spiritual needs. Through working with people who struggle simply to sustain reliable shelter through the winter I have seen humanity in need. This is surely an injustice that I would like to see brought to light and banished from existence. I hope to apply my understanding of this social justice issue in my work as an engineer in the future.

Harrison Neighborhood Association
Andrew Spencer

We don't want to lose focus on this time that we have – Dave Colling
The Fierce Urgency of Now – Rev. Dr. Martin Luther King, Jr.

Story

As Executive Director of Harrison Neighborhood Association (HNA), Dave Colling has the organization's mission statement pinned above his desk: "works to create a prosperous and peaceful community that equitably benefits all of Harrison neighborhood's diverse racial, cultural, and economic groups". However, while the goals contained within the statement are ongoing and continual, HNA's work is very much rooted in the present moment. Thus, Dave likes to think about HNA's work in terms of "how would the community be different if we weren't here?" (D. Collings, personal communication, October 19, 2017). In these terms, the work that HNA are doing right now is the most important in its history.

Conflict:

HNA have experienced great success in the last decade advocating for the development of three different transit extensions that will serve Harrison and its surrounding area. There are going to be three new transit stops in and around Harrison such that every single household in the neighborhood will now be within a ½ mile radius of a station. All of this brings great promise and as well as potential threats to businesses and residents in Harrison.

HNA as an organization also faces similar uncertainty. Before Dave Colling arrived 10 months ago, HNA had three Executive Directors in a 12-month period. This recent turnover means that HNA must now work to regain the trust of local residents, donors, and grant writers.

The transit expansion brings with it pressing issues surrounding the gentrification of the neighborhood that HNA must address. Harrison is receiving a lot of attention from developers which will inevitably lead to home values and rent prices to rise. This is especially problematic for Harrison given that 70% of its residents are renters. Thus, the actions taken by HNA in the years leading up to the transit plans being completed are critical to the lives of many families who have lived in Harrison for generations and represent the life and character of the community. HNA must fight not just on behalf of the residents who now may be forced to move out of their homes, but also to maintain the character of a rich and diverse neighborhood. There are many different directions the neighborhood can take following the extension of transit lines to the area and HNA are positioned to have a large influence over what that looks like.

Decision:

HNA have responded to this urgent need to act with various tactics designed to elevate the voices of Harrison's residents so that their concerns are heard by the city. HNA are actively looking to partner with organizations that aim to help individuals and families avoid being priced out of their homes, and even set them on a path to home ownership. To this end, HNA are partnering with the University of Minnesota's Center for Urban and Regional Affairs (CURA) to survey and research the neighborhood to obtain critical information about home ownership and income. This information will be immensely valuable in discussions with the city concerning the development of the area; it will enable HNA to come prepared with important information about exactly which and how many people are going to be affected by gentrification following the transit expansion. It is especially critical for Harrison to have this information given that city development plans are typically informed by city-wide standards and information, rather than information and survey results from the actual neighborhoods being developed.

As HNA anticipate the fight for equitable development in the areas surrounding the new transit line they are developing an Equity Development Scorecard to be used as a resource to assess proposed development projects. This provides another tool for HNA to use to elevate the voices and concerns of its residents. By having an Equity Development Score for each proposed housing development HNA can make claims to the city that are based in concrete evidence and research that points to whether the developments will be supporting an equitable neighborhood.

HNA also recognize the importance of coalition building and the exercising of collective power. To this end, they have partnered with other groups effected by the Blue Line light-rail transit development to form the Blue Line Coalition (BLC). The BLC operates with the clear goal of promoting development equity in and around the new Blue Line station area plans. Dave Colling and the rest of HNA recognize that even with a strong neighborhood association it can be difficult for areas such as Harrison to have their voice heard at the city government level. Thus, an effective way for them to remedy this is to partner with other stakeholders who share their concerns.

A less direct way that HNA is working to counteract the issues surrounding gentrification in the neighborhood is through an extensive voter turnout campaign. HNA aims to increase voter turnout by 2,000 votes in the next municipal election. Only 28% of the Fifth Ward's (of which Harrison is a part of) 15,000 registered voters voted in this November's general election, by far the lowest voter turnout rate in Minneapolis (Minneapolis Elections and Voter Services). In many respects, this is the most important thing HNA can do to empower its citizens as having a large voting base in Harrison is a good way to ensure that local lawmakers listen to their concerns. Furthermore, this project allows for a sustainable development of power for Harrison's residents; if a culture and infrastructure of high voter turnout is cultivated in Harrison there will be many issues now and, in the future, that Harrison will have an easier job allowing its voice to be heard. For example, the city will be more likely to include affordable housing in their transit development plans if Harrison builds a history of high voter turnout in local elections.

Outcome:

In what is undoubtedly a point of transition in Harrison, much of the future is unknown and lays in the hands of decision-makers at the metro and state level, rather than the neighborhood level. However, HNA is positioned well to influence this decision-making process. It is too early to tell whether the transit projects set to reach Harrison in the next few years will benefit Harrison's residents or force them further out of the city and away from economic opportunity. A lot of this will depend on HNA's leadership for social justice and whether they can harness the collective power of Harrison's residents to ensure an equitable and just future.

Theory

In his article, "Why Stories Matter", Marshall Ganz discusses the importance of stories when it comes to promoting social justice. Ganz highlights how it is essential to have compelling stories of self, us, and now (Ganz, 2009). A good "story of self" (Ganz, 2009, p.2) conveys why one is called to action, what it is about one's life and values that mean one cannot ignore the injustices at hand. A coherent "story of us" (Ganz, 2009, p.3) conveys why a whole community is called to act, based on their shared values and beliefs. All of this must be tied in with a compelling "story of now" that allows a movement to convey the importance of the present moment and how there is a "contradiction between the world as it is and the world as it ought to be" (Ganz, 2009, p.1). Ganz's theory not only accurately describes Harrison Neighborhood Association (HNA), but also prescribes an effective course of action for the organization to generate support and achieve its goals. If HNA can efficaciously convey its stories of now, self and us then they have the potential to build a successful social justice movement that will further their aim of creating an equitable, prosperous and peaceful neighborhood.

HNA have a dynamic "story of self". It is no secret that HNA's past few years have been turbulent on an administrative level. The large amount of turnover at the Executive Director position at HNA has undeniably led to a significant loss of trust among its donors (HNA recently defaulted on one of its grants) and residents of Harrison. Therefore, HNA's story of self is one of an organization that has recently been through difficult times, but is trying to rebuild itself and regain the trust of its stakeholders. It is imperative for this story to be shared with others as it conveys a sense of humility to those HNA are seeking to serve, a crucial step towards building trust. Given this, it will also be helpful for Dave Colling to convey his own "story of self" in order to gain the trust of the community, especially as he is not originally from Harrison. Dave grew up in a poor single-parent household in Detroit and says he aims to use his work to help elevate others out of poverty. Dave also has extensive experience in both government and non-governmental work dating back to his successful management of Keith Ellison's first political campaign in 2006. Thus, there are compelling stories of now for both Dave personally and HNA as an organization. According to Ganz, it is always important for social movements to "claim authorship" (Ganz, 2009, p.2) and share their own stories; this certainly applies to HNA. Without an effective dissemination of their "story of self" it will be difficult to regain the trust of the community.

Building trust in the community is also an essential part of HNA's strategy to combat gentrification in Harrison. HNA are currently working with other organizations (such as CURA) to gather more information about demographics and home ownership in the community; this will allow HNA to be armed with important information about exactly which and how many people are going to be affected by rising housing prices. However, for HNA to be able to gather this information, trust of the community is required. Dave Colling stressed the necessity of building this trust when it comes to conducting survey research like this as residents of Harrison have been surveyed frequently by many different organizations over the years, often with no positive benefits brought back to the community. This adds an additional reason why HNA's "story of self" is so important to convey as it will not just lead to more support for the organization, but also will directly help HNA effectively execute a key part of its strategy.

Linked to this, HNA also has a "story of us" that can "communicate fear, hope, and anxiety" (Ganz, 2009, p.2) and so can help drive people to mobilize and act in support of the organization. HNA recognizes the importance of addressing gentrification not just because of the call to action to help people facing foreclosure, but also because they see the value of maintaining Harrison's rich identity and character. Dave Colling identifies the individuality and uniqueness of Harrison and therefore believes an important part of HNA's mission is to preserve this identity and help Harrison avoid becoming a generic, gentrified neighborhood. It is therefore essential for HNA to convey this "story of us" to potential supporters and establish the connection between this story and the fight to avoid gentrification. This is especially important in this case given that the loss of Harrison's sense of "us" would be the result of planned public transit expansions to the neighborhood. These plans were undoubtedly made with good intentions and, as Dave himself recognized, will bring many benefits to the community. Indeed, HNA played a significant role in advocating for the expansion of public transit to Harrison. Thus, it is likely that many within Harrison or who support HNA will not initially recognize the degree to which the proposed transit plans put Harrison's character and identity at risk. Furthermore, the potential rising housing prices make it clear that not everyone in the community will benefit from the transit developments; thus, part of the story of us for HNA at this time must be to examine who is benefiting and who is being harmed by these plans. This aspect of HNA's "story of us" is particularly essential given that part of their mission is to create a community that "that equitably benefits all of Harrison neighborhood's diverse racial, cultural, and economic groups".

The potential gentrification of Harrison within the next few years provides a compelling "story of now" for HNA. There is serious concern at HNA that many of Harrison's residents, in particular the 72% of residents who are renters (Minnesota Compass), will become priced out of the neighborhood. Given that the city's planned "affordable housing" projects within Harrison will not be built until years after the transit expansions are completed, there is a fierce "urgency of need" (Ganz, 2009, p.1) regarding housing prices within Harrison. This is a problem that must be addressed now as residents will be forced to move immediately if they cannot afford to stay in the neighborhood. Indeed, Executive Director Dave Colling believes that the work undertaken by HNA in the next few years will be as critical to the future of Harrison as any other point in the neighborhood's history. While in the past HNA could take a couple of years off and Harrison would still remain largely the same, right now Dave believes that if HNA were to take "3 or 4 years off and didn't do anything we would come back to a very different neighborhood" (D. Collings, personal communication, October 19, 2017). Thus, the potential increase in housing prices within the neighborhood creates a compelling "story of now" for HNA; this story must be conveyed to generate support for their cause. It will be essential for HNA to explain how the gentrification that may result from the transit expansion would make it difficult for HNA to live up to its mission of creating a community that "equitably" benefits all of Harrison's residents. This story of now must be told by HNA in conjunction with their story of self; this will ensure that residents understand what is at stake, and why it is at stake at this time.

Overall, HNA's compelling and distinct stories of us, self, and now provide a clear example of Marshall Ganz's theory from "Why Stories Matter". Furthermore, all three of these stories, if conveyed effectively, can be used by HNA "to break through the inertia of habit to get people to pay attention" (Ganz, 2009, p.1) to the injustice and inequities surrounding gentrification in Harrison. Thus, Ganz's theory not only accurately describes HNA, but also prescribes an effective course of action for the organization to generate support and achieve their goals. Ganz suggests that all social movements have these compelling stories that are worth being told. The challenge is to articulate and convey these stories in a way that potential supporters will relate to. The subtler challenge for social movements is to actually believe internally that their story is worth telling in the first place (Ganz, 2009, p.2). Most leaders for social justice are not vocationally motivated by power or glory; this can understandably mean that many do not wish to draw attention to themselves or their stories. However, as Ganz argues, these stories of self are essential parts of movement building and so it is crucial for individuals such as Dave or organizations such as HNA to share their story.

Action Plan

A SWOT analysis is be an effective tool to articulate HNA's plan of action going forward. A SWOT analysis, which considers the **S**trengths, **W**eaknesses, **O**pportunities and **T**hreats of an organization or movement, allows HNA to map out where they currently stand, and what lies ahead, in their fight to limit gentrification and maintain Harrison's neighborhood identity. It is essential for Dave Colling and the rest of the team to have an awareness and understanding of these different components of their current situation as it allows for a holistic action plan and ensures that they use their time and resources efficiently and effectively.

HNA's **strengths** were made clear in my meeting with Dave. He brings to the table a wide range of experience in local government, advocacy and organizing, all of which are assets when it comes to seeking to create the type of community and neighborhood that HNA envisions. Furthermore, Dave is a passionate individual who very much appears to live by his values; he wants to make it his mission in life use his work in politics and community organizing to help other people make it out of poverty. Dave is also willing to work collectively with others to achieve shared goals. This is crucial when it comes to advocating for the interests of Harrison. Harrison has historically been a marginalized neighborhood and one way to overcome this is by building broad based coalitions with similar organizations.

HNA are also blessed to have two extremely passionate and knowledgeable individuals as part of its team. Nestor Garcia, a Harrison resident, manages community outreach at HNA. The fact that Nestor is from the community he is serving is a key strength when it comes to community outreach. Nichole Bueller is the program manager at HNA and I was blown away by the knowledge she has about housing and urban planning policies in the Twin Cities. As a licensed attorney, she possesses the attention for detail necessary to analyze city policies effectively. Furthermore, she also possesses the moral imagination to think outside the box as she demonstrated through the various potential solutions to the impending housing crisis she brought up during our brief conversation.

Another one of HNA's strengths is their longevity. HNA have many achievements to show for its 33-year history of working in the community. While HNA's turbulent recent history undoubtedly means that it must work to regain trust from the community, the foundation is there for HNA to be able to build on its long history of working with the community. This history helps HNA engage in essential collective action with others as they can build on their long-lasting relationships. For example, HNA have an extensive partnership with Redeemer Lutheran Church in Harrison, an influential church within the community that places a heavy emphasis on social justice.

If there is one **weakness** currently infringing on HNA's ability to achieve their aims, it is the fallout that has occurred from their recent leadership turnover. The turnover led to a loss of trust in, and therefore funding for, HNA. This clearly has limited the scope of work that HNA can currently undertake, meaning they cannot currently operate on as wide a scale as they would like. However, after witnessing the passion and motivation with which Dave Colling and his team work, I have complete confidence in their ability to overcome these organizational challenges and restore HNA to their full strength in the near future.

HNA have many **opportunities** that can help it address the problem of gentrification in its community. One of these is their compelling story of now. As I previously discussed, HNA's story of now is one that has a clear and urgent call to action for the organization itself, and its supporters. This presents itself as a good opportunity for HNA to make the case to potential donors, grant writers and supporters for why they should support HNA now more than ever.

Additionally, the high visibility of the transit developments within Harrison is also an opportunity for HNA. While the issue of gentrification and rising rent prices is not necessarily a highly visible one, some construction has already begun for the new transit developments in the community. HNA can use the resultant buzz and interest within the community surrounding these construction projects to raise awareness of the consequences of these developments and mobilize support for HNA's cause.

Finally, HNA also have the opportunity to work with many willing collaborators who can help it achieve its goal. As part of the Blue Line Coalition, HNA have strategically placed itself to collectively act with other neighborhood organizations facing similar issues and concerns. The fact that there are other organizations in similar positions willing to act in collaboration is certainly an opportunity that Dave Colling and HNA are seizing. Furthermore, HNA have successfully embraced the opportunity to collaborate with CURA, an organization willing to work with HNA to provide them with crucial research and data.

When it comes to fighting off gentrification in the community, disinterest for the issue among the Harrison community and public poses a significant **threat**. Gentrification is not an issue that is entirely visible until it is too late, and is not always associated with public transit expansions. Indeed, when most hear about the expansion of public transit, little regard is given to the type negative consequences that

Dave and HNA are working to avoid. The presence of this threat makes it even more important for HNA to stress what is at stake here: the livelihood of many in the community, as well as Harrison's heart and soul.

Another threat facing HNA is the scale of decision making when it comes to affordable housing and transit expansion. Most of the decisions regarding transit and housing in Harrison are made at a city government level, and thus by forces more powerful than HNA. Therefore, a threat to HNA's work is ambivalence about the actual issues facing Harrison residents by those who hold the power in this situation. This was demonstrated by the exasperation Dave and Nichole felt when only a short paragraph was dedicated to the issue of housing prices and affordable housing in the city government's strategic plan for the transit expansion in Harrison. In this case, the city planners were either unaware or did not care about the most important issues facing the Harrison neighborhood; this poses a threat to HNA given the power the city government holds in the decision-making process.

As I reflect on what I have learnt profiling HNA up to this point, what keeps coming back to me is Dave Colling's belief that to do good work in the community one must always be asking themselves "how would the community be different if we weren't here?" (D. Collings, personal communication, October 19, 2017). This inevitably warrants a strong focus on a community's "story of now", which is something HNA are certainly doing through their prioritizing of the issue of gentrification. While keeping housing prices affordable and maintaining Harrison's character will be no easy task, I have full confidence that the team at HNA have the energy and the focus to put Harrison in the best position possible going forward.

Works Cited

Final Results Minneapolis 2017 General Election. *Minneapolis Elections and Voter Services*. Retrieved from http://vote.minneapolismn.gov/www/groups/public/@clerk/documents/webcontent/2017-results-general.pdf

Ganz, M. (2009, March 1). Why Stories Matter: The Art Craft of Social Change. Sojourners Magazine.

Neighborhood data & trends for Harrison. *Minnesota Compass*. Retrieved from http://www.mncompass.org/profiles/neighborhoods/minneapolis/harrison

About the Author – Andrew Spencer

I am a sophomore double majoring in Justice and Peace Studies and Political Science. I am driven by the knowledge that every person has inner value, beauty, and agency. I am inspired by the vast number of people across the world working to make a difference and my research into Harrison Neighborhood Association has shown me the different avenues through which equity can be sought.

Headwaters Foundation for Justice
Sofía Leyva

"What makes this model really special, to me, is that it disrupts the traditional philanthropic model...
Donor > Foundation > Organization > Community
...replacing it with one in which the Community plays every role which, in turn, increases both engagement and accountability. Over the course of six months, we learned from each other in workshops on race and class, grassroots fundraising, site visits, and, finally, grant making." - Cohort One Participant.

Story

"Philanthropy sucks," David Nicholson looked at me from across the table and laughed. "My buddy told me that philanthropy sucks but there's this one place called Headwaters where they kind of let you do whatever you want." I guess I wasn't expecting the executive director of a philanthropic foundation to be saying the words "philanthropy sucks."

Headwaters Foundation for Justice works to make philanthropy accessible to all with a firm belief that those who are directly affected by injustice are best suited to make decisions on where resources are needed.

At an information session for Headwaters' upcoming Giving Project, an alumna reflected on her transformative experience with community grantmaking: "when I think of philanthropy I think of rich, white men. I think of the McKnight's and the Carnegies of the world. I didn't think that philanthropy could mean me too. I didn't know that people who looked like me could do philanthropy." It was through these words that the apprehensive feelings towards philanthropy were articulated. Traditional philanthropy can feel exclusive. It can feel institutional and discriminatory. Traditional philanthropy has become another way for privileged persons to control resources.

Headwaters Foundation for Justice was formed on a platform where funding decisions are placed in the hands of the community because "philanthropy sucks" when the faces of those who hold, award, and compete for resources don't match those who are facing injustice.

Before I started my internship at Headwaters, I knew nothing about fundraising and grantmaking. I considered myself an activist. I attended rallies, protests, and demonstrations. I advocated against injustices on campus. I didn't think about the role of money and social justice. Money was the product of corporate greed and capitalism. Money was institutionalized and very scarce for social justice causes. Headwaters Foundation confronts these barriers that we face with money by educating community members on the dynamics of power between race, class, and money in society and by encouraging individuals to fundraise and engage in community grantmaking.

Headwaters Foundation for Justice has defined themselves as a leader in community organizing in philanthropy. One way that they do this is through The Giving Project. The Giving Project is a six-month program that takes twenty-five individuals and creates a cross-race, cross-class cohort. These individuals participate in race and class workshops where they analyze the relationship between race, class, and power when it comes to money and fundraising. They then fundraise money, pool their dollars, and make collective decisions on where to award grants.

In 2017, over the course of six months, twenty-five participants in a cross-class, cross-race cohort raised over $215,000. These participants reviewed grant applications from organizations across the

Twin Cities and Greater Minnesota. This cohort of twenty-five individuals collectively made the decision to award 9 organizations with two-year grants of $10,000. Over the course of six months, an intersectional group of individuals took back, and democratized, philanthropy.

Of course, those six months of work require six months of recruitment, advertising, and preparation. As soon as the summer months come to a close, staff at Headwaters immediately gets the ball rolling with preparation for the Giving Project. All staff members play an active role in recruitment for the program and the Giving Project is spearheaded by program officer, Allison Johnson Heist.

Allison Johnson Heist joined the Headwaters' staff in January 2015 as a Ron McKinley Philanthropy Fellow. She brought the model of the Giving Project to Headwaters as a way to turn community individuals into social justice philanthropists. Headwaters' program is modeled after Giving Projects that run through Social Justice Fund Northwest—although Headwaters has ways to make them unique. Many other Giving Projects that run throughout the country keep a specific focus, for example, Social Justice Fund runs Giving Projects that center around gender, environment, criminal, or racial justice. Headwaters Foundation runs their program in a slightly different way; one Giving Project is run per year and all the diverse interests are placed within one cohort to create a more intersectional group. Over the past three years, Allison has successfully run three different Giving Projects at Headwaters that have raised over $300,000 in grants for justice organizations, brought in over 200 new donors to Headwaters, and significantly impacted the Minnesota community.

The work of the Giving Project doesn't end after six months, either. Headwaters follows up with organizations one year after awarding them grants to see how the funds were used— Headwaters gives out general operating grants because they don't believe they have wisdom to tell organizations where resources are needed most. Alumni of the Giving Project continue to carry the skills they gained from relational fundraising and community grantmaking: one particular alumna from cohort 3, is now the Program Officer and Grants Manager at the Women's Foundation of Minnesota. She has been able to use her experience with the Giving Project to propose ideas for grassroots grantmaking within her foundation and advocate for community grantmaking. A cohort 1 alumna now works at Eureka! Recycling. She has started a people of color caucus to lift up the voices of people of color. This was an idea that she took directly from the Giving Project, which hosts a white and POC caucus to explore the roles of white people and people of color in the justice world.

Through the Giving Project, Headwaters Foundation has been able to mark itself as a leader in the philanthropic community. Recently, the AAPIP (Asian Americans/Pacific Islanders in Philanthropy) announced Headwaters as a new member in their organization. This was a significant moment for Headwaters as they strive to make themselves more known throughout the philanthropic community.

Theory

A large way in which Headwaters Foundation uplifts the voices of the community and utilizes collective decision-making is through the Giving Project. The program builds power in the community, advocates leadership development, and funds social change—all through the power of community individuals. By transforming the traditional model of philanthropy, Headwaters works to democratize leadership—in other words, Headwaters opens philanthropic participation to a more widespread group and supports the voices of community members when making collective decisions.

The Giving Project is central to Headwaters' idea that those who experience injustice have the most wisdom and knowledge of where resources are most needed. By involving community members from different backgrounds along with past and current grantees, they are supporting the voices of the communities they are serving. They are moving leadership from the traditional philanthropy of one person who is distanced from the injustice model, to leadership characterized by an array of diverse voices that are impacted by injustices. Headwaters democratizes the process of philanthropy through the Giving Project as they allow the cohort to collectively discuss and make decisions on where funds will be awarded.

Headwaters Foundation works through democratizing leadership, not only within their programs, but also in their work with other foundations. Recently, Headwaters hosted a group of program officers from different foundations in Minnesota to learn about community grantmaking. Program Officers Allison Johnson Heist and Melissa Rudnick from Headwaters led a discussion around how to close the gap between who is making funding decisions and who is benefiting from the funds. Allison and Melissa implemented their theories of democratizing leadership by educating other philanthropists so that they too could take collective action to democratize their foundations and leaders.

Headwaters' priority is to advance equity to end injustice. Their purpose is to facilitate the voices of those who experience injustice because they have the wisdom to locate resources, to make decisions on funding priorities, and take collective action. This in itself is democratizing leadership. Headwaters Foundation strives to leave a legacy of change and transformation in the community through democratizing leadership.

Action Plan

The Giving Project is a fairly new collective action that has been embraced by the staff at Headwaters Foundation. Brought to the organization three years ago by Allison Johnson Heist, the program circulates energy from all staff—not just the program team.

Recruitment for the program takes up the brunt of the work for the whole staff. This is time consuming and carefully thought out. This is part of their strategic grassroots organizing. When recruiting for the program, the process is very similar to fundraising with current and prospective donors: individual calls are made and relationships with individuals are formed. Prospective participants for this program come directly from the diverse communities of Minnesota. After recruitment, the cohort is formed and through a process of education on fundraising, race/class workshops, and grassroots organizing the cohort builds their own community. They then use their skills in grassroots organizing and community philanthropy to practice capacity building.

The collective action of the Giving Project is central to the mission of Headwaters to amplify the power of the community to advance equity and justice. Headwaters Foundation works to democratize the leadership of philanthropy and does so through this Giving Project. The funding decisions are literally placed in the hands of twenty-five members of the community who award grants after receiving the resources they need from Headwaters.

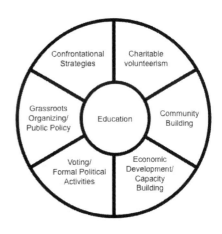

After three successful runs of the Giving Project, and as her fellowship comes to an end, Headwaters has decided to keep Allison as a full-time staff. The Giving Project has increased dollars significantly and brought in hundreds of new donors to Headwaters. More importantly, the Giving Project has educated individuals on the process of grassroots organizing for change and has given them the ability to use capacity building within their own lives and justice groups.

As Headwaters continues to develop the Giving Project model, the demand for the program will continue to expand. Already, there has been demand for more than one program per year and questions about an all-alumni Giving Project. In order to make these programs a reality, Headwaters will need to find resources to expand their program staff to accommodate the extra workload. Each Giving Project is unique in its own way and requires careful planning, attention, and care from the facilitators involved. The grassroots, community-building model is implemented in each step as staff create relationships during the recruitment process and continue to work closely with individuals after they complete the program. Individuals are carefully considered before being invited into a Giving Project cohort to create a diverse, vibrant, healthy community.

This growth may come within the next few years at Headwaters. During my short time as an intern for the foundation, two new staff were hired bringing the total number of employees to nine. A new development team was created to process gifts and focus on fundraising. Growth is constantly happening at Headwaters as programs develop and new relationships with donors are formed. As the foundation continues to make itself known in the philanthropic community, community grantmaking will also, hopefully, continue to be a more widespread action.

Works Cited

Headwaters Foundation for Justice. (2018, January 04). Retrieved September, 2017, from https://headwatersfoundation.org/
Klein, Mike. (2016). *Democratizing Leadership: Counter-Hegemonic Democracy in Communities, Organizations, and Institutions.* Charlotte, NC: Information Age Publishing.
Nicholson, David. Executive Director at Headwaters Foundation for Justice [Personal communication]. (2016, October 19).

About the Author - Sofía Leyva

As an upper middle class, white-passing woman, I feel I have a responsibility to use my privileges to challenge current systems of marginalization and inequity in our society and here at the University of St. Thomas. I am currently working towards an undergraduate degree in Justice and Peace Studies with a minor in Non-Profit Management. I see my education as a way to supplement the justice work that I pursue outside of the classroom, and my internship at Headwaters Foundation has been transformative of the way I view and approach the realm of social justice.

Hope for Tomorrow
Katelyn Zelenka

*I am a unique person with my
own special talents, interests, hopes, and dreams.
My journey is my own—
where I have been, where I want to go.
I am responsible for how I travel the road I am on,
the choices I make, and the paths I take.
My journey is what I make of it!*

Hope for Tomorrow, 2017

Story

"You are going to change the future by working with the youth" (Peterson, 2017). Karen, the chair of Hope for Tomorrow (HFT), has a deep connection with the program. After having a rough upbringing, Karen became a mentor to teach adolescents that no matter what struggles they are going through, they can do whatever they want and make something out of their lives. She expressed that as a child, there was no one to tell her that she had the potential to pursue her dream of becoming a teacher and that she, herself, did not believe that she could do anything like that. Karen asserts that "It doesn't matter if your dad was in jail, it doesn't matter because I made the decision on how I was going to live my life. Kids have to know that they have that decision, it doesn't matter what the circumstances are" (Peterson, 2017). Karen also believes that everyone needs a mentor in their life; "someone that you can trust and talk to and you don't feel that they are going to judge you, but might explain things to you and just have conversions with" (Peterson, 2017). This is what HFT aims to do.

There are people to take care of the students who excel and there are people to take care of the students who don't, but there is no one to help the students who are in the middle, Karen explains. HFT identifies students who care about school and could benefit from a positive role model that would help them reinforce critical life skills. When asked why mentoring is important, Karen answered that "People ask, 'Are these at-risk kids?'. Well, in 2017, every kid is at risk in my opinion and everyone can benefit from a mentor, not just 8th graders; good kids, awesome kids, bad kids, adults, we all have mentors in our lives" (Peterson, 2017). When I spoke with Kayla, a mentee who became a mentor, she stated that "Some people don't have those kinds of role models; whether their mom has passed away or their mom is not in the picture, or not being who they should be. I think just having a strong, successful woman in their life just shows them that they can do the same" (Auers, 2017). Kayla, like Karen, came from a broken home. Her mother was an alcoholic and was in and out of the picture. Kayla admitted that "It was really hard to grow up with an alcoholic parent" but HFT allowed her to "come out of my shell more" and "connect with people better" (Auers, 2017).

HFT Life Skills

Lifelong Learning
Building and Displaying Confidence
Work Skills
    Punctuality
    Accountability
    Getting along with co-workers
    Appreciating the benefits of diversity
    Contributing to a team effort
Communication and Interpersonal Skills
    Oral and Written Communication
    Building rapport and empathy
    Effective and active listening
Personal Skills
    Maintaining a healthy body and mind
    Coping with and managing emotions
    Stress management
    Prioritizing and time management

Relationship and People Skills
    Respecting the individuality and strength of others
    Being able to form, nurture and maintain friendships
    Being a responsible citizen
    Being a good role model
Leadership Skills
    Being organized and accountable
    Problem solving
    Decision making
    Goals setting and action planning

HFT's curriculum is grounded in the empowerment of young teens in order to help them realize their full personal and academic potential. They achieve this by focusing on teaching life skills. Karen asserts that "you are not learning life skills, no one is telling you to shake someone's hand when you meet them and look someone in the eye and speak clearly" (Peterson, 2017). Life skills, shown in Figure 1, are essential because, "We live in a social environment where the ability to interact, cope with change and stress, learn, communicate, problem solve, manage time and build confidence are the basis for getting along with others, reaching our goals and living a happy and healthy life" (Hope for Tomorrow, 2017). One skill taught in the first session of the program is standing when speaking. Kayla described that "I was always terrified of public speaking, I hated it, and I think that somehow I gained confidence from doing that...I think they wanted to instill that 'we want you to be a successful woman someday' and I think that is something that I took from it" (Auers, 2017).

Another thing that HFT aims to do is show the opportunities available to all students; they do this through taking mentees on field trips. One of the field trips is to a place of employment, which is meant to show mentees that within one workplace, there are many jobs that require all different types of skills. The other is to a postsecondary educational institution. Karen explains that "The point of the college tour is to open your eyes to the fact that, well gosh, regardless of what is happening in your house anyone can go to college and you just have to work hard and you can do it" (Peterson, 2017). I asked Kayla to explain an experience that affected her during her time as a mentee in HFT and she stated that the college tour was very valuable to her. She expressed that it "just expanded your mind, like there are going to be so many opportunities outside of my little 8th-grade mind" (Auers, 2107).

The program stays with mentees. Kayla admitted that "It could have been just small things that I learned in there that I didn't necessarily know affected me as much as it did, but really did help me grow as a person" (Auers, 2017). The relationship that is built between mentee and mentor is strong and lasts a lifetime. Kayla voiced that she still meets with her mentor every three to six months and was recently invited to her mentor's family Thanksgiving. HFT also instills acceptance. Karen offers that HFT teaches mentees that everyone has different things going on in their lives and that no one is perfect, but there are different opportunities for everyone. She offers that "You are going to change the future by working with the youth…they are impressionable and that is the age that they are learning. This is where we can make a change, we can make a change in the social environment by teaching respect, by teaching friendship" (Peterson, 2107).

Theory

HFT focuses on the empowerment of teens through the empowerment of mentors. Starting as a social movement organization (SMO) and recently transitioning into a non-profit organization, HFT has developed an organizational strategy of leadership that gives power to the mentors while still maintaining structure through a board of directors. This organizational strategy is strongly linked to the Human Resource frame created by Bolman and Deal (2008). Frames "are maps that aid navigation, and tools for solving problems and getting things done" (Bolman & Deal, 2008, P. 16). Bolman and Deal created these frames in order to "know what you are up against and what you can do about it." (2008, P. 11) It is like putting all of your tools into a tool belt so you know what skills you have and what your capabilities are.

Bolman and Deal created four different frames that have been identified through studying different organizations. The four frames that they created were Structural, Human Resource, Political, and Symbolic (Bolman & Deal, 2008). I have identified HFT as the Human Resource frame. Bolman and Deal describe this frame as a family with their central concepts being needs, skills, and relationships (2008). Within this frame, the image of leadership is centered around empowerment though aligning organizational and human needs (Bolman & Deal, 2008). With HFT's transition from an SMO to a non-profit, the threat of becoming a heavily hierarchical organization becomes real. Mike Klein purposed a solution to this constant pressure that SMOs may feel. Defined as the suspension between the "initial and final extremes" in order to sustain a democratic structure that promotes a creative and artistic space for leadership to grow, normative communitas allows for an organization to remain democratic while still organized (Klein, 2017, P.13). Through Bolman and Deal's Human Resource frame and Klein's Creative Tensions in Social Movement Organizations, HFT's leadership can be explained.

At the heart of the Human Resource frame are the central concepts of: needs, skills, and relationships (Bolman & Deal, 2008). HFT relies on these concepts to shape leadership within their organization. Most of the mentors bring their personal experiences into the program that translate into skills. With the challenging childhood that Kayla and Karen both faced, they are able to share their stories and lead with experiences that others may not have. These personal experiences are assets because others can relate to them which generates trust and the growth of relationships. When relationships are built, needs can be communicated and met which invokes better leadership. Bolman and Deal stress the importance of empowerment in leadership. HFT does this by promoting volunteers from within the organization. After being a mentor for some time, volunteers are able to run for the lead mentor. Each lead mentor is voted in by the other mentors in their chapter, which continues the role of empowerment in leadership. Also, to open a new chapter, mentors have to volunteer for a minimum of one year. Empowerment of leadership is necessary within this because mentors have to make the decision to open a new chapter and propose the HFT program to the sponsoring school and get it approved while being confident that they have other mentors to rely on. Through this, leaders are cultivated in the ground of the current work. As empowerment grows, relationships can flourish. Most of the new mentors hear about HFT through word-of-mouth. Relationships are essential because of this. With the threat of bureaucratization, HFT's main source of growth is vulnerable.

Klein addresses this threat of bureaucratization in his article "Creative Tensions in Social Movement Organizations" (2017) and proposes to combat it by sustaining a normative communitas. As HFT recently moved from being an SMO to a non-profit organization, they face new guidelines as a non-profit. With these new guidelines, the importance of relationships dwindles. Klein proposes that social movement organizations (SMOs) have four key characteristics and as the organization transitions into a bureaucratic organization, they transform into four new characteristics, seen below:

With the left side being the characteristics of an SMO and right side being characteristics of a bureaucracy, the fight between a democratic and hierarchical structure is apparent. Klein offers that collaboration

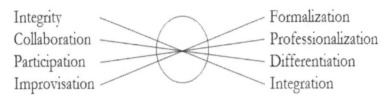

Creative Tensions in Social Movement Organizations Klein, 2017, P.14)

and differentiation are at odds with each other, though the use of "minimized role differentiation" or redundancy provide a way alleviate the tension (Klein, 2017, P. 15). HFT has done some of this by only having a board of directors, lead mentors, and mentors. With only three levels of leadership, there is less risk of leadership transitioning into a hierarchal structure. HFT has a leadership structure with built-in redundancies. Klein uses the metaphor of a bridge design to explain this. Redundancies are built into a bridge's design in order to account for weaknesses or failures. If one piece of the bridge - or a person in an organization - fails, redundancies keep the bridge from collapsing after something happens - or redundancies in leadership roles allow for another person to pick up where the other left off (Klein, 2017). Through redundancy in roles, leadership in HFT has sustained a democratic structure.

Understanding leadership and what it looks like in an organization is important in order to prepare for future challenges and to be resilient. With the frame provided by Bolman and Deal, an organization can identify central concepts that drive leadership and how those concepts can be turned into assets. This identification helps construct a set of tools that can be used to overcome those future challenges. When combined with the implementation of a normative communitas, an organization can strengthen their leadership while remaining democratic. Fighting off institutionalization is important in order to sustain the movement's mission and foster growth for leadership. As HFT continues to grow, leadership will need to preserve creative tensions between the energy and agency of their grassroots work, and the structure and resources necessary to sustain their work into the future.

Action Planning

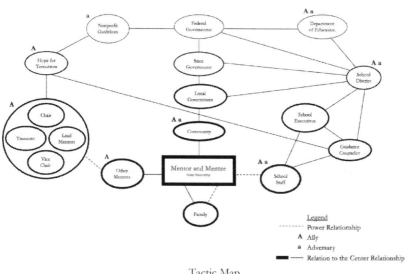

Tactic Map

Defined by Douglas Johnson and Nancy Pearson, "Tactical mapping is a method of visualizing the relationships and institutions that surround..." us (2009, P. 92). This technique allows us to look at all of the relationships that are involved in an organization in order to create "a picture that represents a social space" (Johnson & Pearson, 2009, P. 92). Once the relationships within an organization are understood, "decisions are made, incentives are given or taken away, and actions are taken" (Johnson & Pearson, 2009, P. 92). While piecing together a tactical map, key relationships and power dynamics may become apparent when they may have been overlooked if one was not constructed.

When starting a tactical map, the first thing that is identified is the center relationship. This is usually the direct, "face to face" relationship that has the most impact on the institution or relationship that is being looked at. In HFT, I identified the center relationship to be between the mentor and the mentee, shown in Figure 4. This relationship is at the core of the organization; everything that happens depends on a relationship between the mentor and the mentee. The next step after identifying the center relationship is to find other everyday relationships that both people in the center relationship experience. Other mentors, school staff, the community, and family were the everyday relationships that I saw impacted the center relationship the most. To continue building the tactical map, I looked for relationships that may not be in contact with the center relationship on an everyday basis, but still have a trickle-down impact. I found HFT's Board of Directors, local government, school executives, and the school's guidance counselor to be the next step of relationships. Then I went one step further out and identified the government groups and institutions that had an effect on the center relationship. Here I recognized HFT, the state and federal government, the school district, the Department of Education, and Nonprofit guidelines. The center relationship hardly ever is in contact with these institutions, but they have a major impact on the relationship. I represented these relationships on the diagram by the thickness of the border surrounding the person. For example, the further the relationship is from the center relationship, the thinner the line.

Along with identifying institutions and people that have an effect on the center relationship, a tactical map categorizes these as allies, adversaries, and power relationships. Johnson and Pearson state "Determining the nature of relationships provides insight into potential tactics" (2009, P. 95). Shown in the diagram, the people or institutions that have an "**A**" are allies and "**a**" are adversaries. I also depicted power relationships by adding a dashed line (- - - - -) connecting the individuals.

"Good strategy is based on three sources of knowledge: knowing your adversary, knowing yourself, and knowing the terrain" (Johnson & Pearson, 2009, P. 92). Once the tactical map was finished, I identified which people or institutions were allies, adversaries, or both. HFT's leadership presents as allies towards the core relationship because, without the support of the mentees, there would be no need for the organization. The school's guidance counselor is also an ally. They have the most knowledge of which students would benefit the most from participating in the program, making them an effective ally and a power relationship. I decided that the nonprofit guidelines present as adversaries because they enforce rules on what HFT is and is not able to do. For the same reason, I believe that the federal, state, and local government could present as an adversary. Although, they do provide funding and tax exemptions that help nonprofit organizations like HFT gain money (maybe some other way of saying this?) The Department of Education and the School District could be either allies or adversaries depending on the rules they put in place and the funding that they give to the school. Similar to that, school staff and executives could present as both allies and adversaries because of the possibility of them not allowing HFT to operate in their school.

I found the most important power relationship to be between the mentee and the school staff, specifically the school guidance counselor. The guidance counselor is the individual that chooses what students participate in the HFT program, leaving them to decide who they thought would benefit the most from the curriculum. The next power relationship that I found was between the mentees and their family. The HFT program begins with the parents of the mentee allowing their child to participate in HFT; if this does not happen, the center relationship does not exist. Another power relationship I identified was between the Board of Directors and the mentors. This relationship is dependent upon the Board of Directors approving the wants and needs of the mentors and remaining true to HFT's mission.

As stated before, once a tactical map is developed, decisions can be made and actions can be taken. Based on the tactical map and the experience that I have with HFT, I recommend that the organization should strengthen their relationship with the community that they have chapters in. By doing this, I believe that they will have more of an impact on the mentee and will potentially get local community members to volunteer as mentors. Another product that could come from gaining a better relationship with the community is the possibility of more donations to the organization and better attendance and acceptance of the program. As the connection with communities grow, HFT will be able to fine-tune their curriculum to maximize the impact that it has on the mentee. Once that happens, more youths will have access to the support and tools that they need.

Works Cited

Auers, M. (2017, October 30). Personal Interview with K. Zelenka.

Bolman, L., & Deal, T. (2008). Reframing organizations artistry, choice, and leadership / Lee G.

Bolman, Terrence E. Deal. (4th ed., Jossey-Bass business & management series). San Francisco: Jossey-Bass.

Hope for Tomorrow. (2017). Retrieved October 10, 2017, from http://hopefortomorrowmentoring.org

Johnson, D. A., & Pearson, N. L. (2009). Tactical Mapping: How Nonprofits Can Identify the Levers of Change. The Nonprofit Quarterly, 92-99. Retrieved from www.npqmag.org

Klein, M. (2017). Creative Tensions in Social Movement Organizations. Unpublished manuscript, used with permission of the author.

Peterson, K. (2017, October 12). Personal Interview with K. Zelenka.

About the Author - Katelyn Zelenka

I am from…

I am from being a sister and adamantly trying to teach my younger sisters that they are all powerful and all knowing.

I was from a small town in rural Minnesota where I felt trapped, but now I am from the big city of Minneapolis where I feel free.

I am from the short trip to Europe that ignited my strong desire to travel and love for going on adventures.

I from all of my experiences that have shaped me into the resilient, beautiful, and smart woman that I am today.

Line Break Media
Sam Miner

Story

After talking with one fourth of the current owners of Line break media, Erick Boustead, I was able to comprehend a more cohesive story to the rise and creation of Line Break Media. Erick Boustead was born and raised in the Northwoods of Wisconsin, and then later moved to the Twin Cities to go to school and follow his passion of music. While he was growing up he and his friends would often film themselves skateboarding or playing music. In high school he recorded a short music video. From an early age he was collaborating with other artists, musicians and even activists. He challenged cultural narratives before he even understood what strategic communications was.

His passion for bringing people together and mixing the arts was eventually translated into event planning, where he and Nolan Morice, another current owner of Line Break, would bring local artists, musicians and activists together to perform and create. After doing this for a while he and Nolan ended up a little burnt out, however, in the process they managed to network with a lot of organizations around the Twin Cities and made plenty of soon to be helpful connections.

After meeting with many of these organizations they realized what a lot of people lacked yet needed in the social justice community, video. Media justice was lacking in many of the organizations they were in contact with. They saw this problem and recognized that they had an answer to it. Their first video that they created for an organization was for Voices for Racial Justice. They interviewed a lot of their alumni, captured b roll, which is extra footage that enhances your story and adds another visual dimension, and eventually put together their first video. From there they only expanded.

Line Break continued meeting with organizations working for social justice to find out what was needed and how their work could contribute to or enhance the work of these activists. Digital single-lens reflex (DSLR) cameras were just starting to become more popular and accessible and it seemed like the world of media justice and multimedia communication was starting to rapidly expand. By this time Line Break had decided that they wanted to produce compelling content, provide training for video and editing, and teach communication strategy workshops, all of which they are still currently doing.

Their main mission, however, is to create compelling and moving video content for organizations doing the actual work for social justice, in order to provoke a larger and broader audience to take action or support the cause. They accomplish this through the storytelling method. This allows them to convey messages through testimonials and lived experiences and portray the organization or movement in way that a larger audience can relate and connect to. Since video is obviously very focused on images, it allows the viewer to really conceptualize something that may be complex or hard to explain otherwise. Communication is one of Line Break's main jobs. Through many different facets of their work they effectively communicate with the public much of the tangible work that these social justice organizations are trying so hard to accomplish. They are the microphone to the talent.

Line Break is a worker owned cooperative, which is essentially run in a horizontal power structure. There are four co-owners, Erick Boustead, Nolan Morice, Eleonore Wesserle and Majid Jamaleldine. They have differing roles within the organization but equally contribute and equally share in the decision making process. They participate in weekly staff meetings, annual and semi-annual retreats and work together to come to conclusions and formulate new ideas for improvement.

When it comes to the relationship between them and their clients they most commonly use agreements called MOU's, which stands for memorandum of understanding. This form clearly lays out what they are planning on doing and how they will be contributors to their organization. While these are formal documents that lay out their role, Line Break also considers the client to be the executive producer, so, ultimately whatever the client says goes. Line Break tries to push what they believe is the most effective and strategic way to tell the specific organization's story, however, sometimes at the counter-position of their client. Often times when it comes to nonprofits, who have certain obligations to say and present things in a specific way, Line Break has to recognize this and allow the client to do what they feel is the best way to convey their message. Ultimately, Line Break wants to be a tool for these organizations and they understand the importance of compromise.

Line Break has currently worked with over 150 different organizations nationally and plan on continuing their reach. Erick is now living on the east coast across the river from New York City, where he often shoots video. He's in one of the biggest cities in the United States which allows him to expand and to reach a more national level, as well as cover things that might not be accessible in the Twin Cities. The organization plans to continue creating content for movements and organizations, however, Erick sees himself creating web series in the future, broadening his range of content that could grab the attention of viewers in a different, or even more entertaining way, while still providing compelling ideas and provoking insight into the nation's social justice organizations (E. Boustead, Personal Interview, 2017).

Line break stepped up and filled the role as mediator for the community of social justice work. While the actual social justice work being done around the Twin Cities, when it comes to social justice issues, is incredibly important, they still need a light to be shed on them in order to create a broader reach and instill support for their cause.

Theory

In order for an organization to be successful, it needs to be intentional. In order to be intentional it needs to have tools and resources. Storytelling is a powerful tool, one that is frequently undervalued when referring to big social movements and the creation of influential organizations. What people tend to forget is that every organization and everyone within that organization has a story and they all deserve to be shared in some outlet or another. These stories may not be fully developed and could potentially grow every day. Regardless, these stories can be told. Marshall Ganz gives us a formula for storytelling. He starts by claiming a story of self, which is simply defined as the experiences and values of an individual that have called them to serve. Like most of his model, this part of a story is malleable. Because everyone's story is so different, the way in which they choose to share it varies as well. Everyone has something that motivates them to do what they do, and a story of self gets at the heart of a person's intentions through their experiences and values.

Once someone begins to understand an individual's story of self, they can start to formulate a story of us. If specifically relating to an organization, a story of us is defined by Marshall Ganz as the communication of, "values and experiences that a community, organization, campaign or movement shares and what capacity or resources that community of "us" has to accomplish its goals" (Ganz). These are shared experiences within an organization that push them to continue doing the work that they do. Often times these experiences and collective values bring participants of the organization together and merge stories of selves. A story of us is important to creating cohesion throughout a movement or organization.

Finally, Ganz describes a story of now in his storytelling formula. The story of now is the urgent challenge that we are called upon to tackle. It includes not only the challenge but also the reason that someone is called to act upon it. The story of self and the story of us begin the path that leads to the creation of the story of now. The combination of the three stories manage to be linear while simultaneously reshaping themselves iteratively. All organizations have stories, but not all organizations make their stories, and other's stories, their focus.

Line Break media appreciates and enhances other organizations' stories of self, us, and now, while still staying true to their own. Erick Boustead, a part owner, shared his story of self with me. From an early age he was passionate about video, community collaboration, and communication. He challenged cultural narratives before he even knew what strategic communication was. His past experiences shaped his decision to work for social justice in a new and innovative way. Once he started networking with other people who shared his interests and other organizations who needed his skills, Line Break was able to begin their story of us. Line Break communicated with social justice organizations across the Twin Cities and found out what was missing or what these organizations needed. Video and strategic communication was at the forefront of their needs. Line Break had the tools to create compelling and authentic videos to raise awareness for and tell the stories of these organizations that were doing tangible work to promote social justice.

Storytelling proves its importance when it is able to galvanize a larger audience and convince a group of people to join a movement. Line Break recognizes that power and uses it in their work with organizations. They are continuing this effort and calling themselves to do more in their story of now. Line Break has worked with over roughly 150 organizations, creating compelling videos and promoting their work. They have plans to continue growing and expanding their reach. They now have a location in New York City, an area that is never short of national and powerful movements. Additionally, Line Break hopes to provide even more pathways and outlets for activism media. Erick Boustead mentioned his passion for creating a web series that would broaden his range of content and could grab the attention of viewers in a different, or more entertaining way, while still providing compelling ideas and provoking insight into the nation's social justice organizations.

Line Break exemplifies leadership for social justice through its innovative methods for sharing stories of self, us, and now. They are doing what others can't do themselves and broadening the reach of organizations through telling their stories in a clear and convincing way. Compelling stories are interwoven in every organization working for social justice and Line Break is able to lead by sharing these stories.

Action Plan

Line Break media is committed to working towards social change. The best way to analyze their work is to approach it through the lens of the Social Change Wheel. The spokes on the Social Change Wheel are a comprehensive spectrum of strategies that are used in order to create social change. Line Break does not integrate all of them into their organization but every spoke that they do have moves in harmony with one another and works to continue improvement.

Line Break started with community building and have continued to maintain that mission throughout their growth. This spoke on their wheel combines well with their connections to grassroots organizing. Before Line Break was even created, part owners, Erick Boustead and Nolan Morice were meeting grassroots organizations and

members of their community through event planning. They built upon their community and formed connections that they maintain still today. These initial strategies lay their foundation for social change. The base of their commitment to social change stems from education within media.

The organization's number one goal is to educate those who are not yet informed on a certain social justice led organization's mission. They achieve this through the creation of thought provoking and inspiring content that forces their audience to pay attention and oftentimes to act. Not only does Line Break strive to educate through their own persuasive content, they have also incorporated programs to teach others how to create their own effective media. They sponsor workshops and training programs that teach a lot of the work they do themselves. This type of direct service is vital in creating more people that feel confident in using media as a way to incite social change.

In many cases, the information Line Break provides to its communities leads to political action and even capacity building, two more spokes of the wheel. Some of Line Break's content is trying to incite direct action from their intended audiences. This could mean to vote for an upcoming bill that promotes the objectives and general well-being of a social justice led organization. These calls to action could also be to participate or donate to these causes, allowing for more people to become capacity builders themselves. Line Break's videos have a message they want to send and an outcome they hope to receive. The outcomes may be visible in many different ways, but they all encompass hopes for social change.

Education is the most important and potent part of the Social Change Wheel for Line Break. It stands at the center of the wheel with the other spokes such as community building, grassroots organizing, direct action, political action, and capacity building circling around it, maintaining cohesiveness. An organization is successful when the Social Change Wheel is comprehensive and concurrent. Line Break leads by example when it comes to education through media. In order to continue to build upon this I think expanding their reach and growing in size could be a useful way to extend their influence. Education spreads through a web of relationships and if Line Break continues to weave this web, they can encourage social change on an even larger scale than they do now.

Works Cited

Ganz, Marshall. "350.Org Workshops." *350org Workshops*, archive.workshops.350.org/toolkit/story/#storyofus.

Klein, M. (2017). Social change wheel analysis: Beyond the dichotomy of charity or justice, in Colon, C.; Gristwood, A. & Woolf, M. (2017). Civil Rights and Inequalities, Occasional Publication #6, Boston: CAPA, The Global Education Network.

Line Break Media, Design Action Collective, linebreakmedia.org/about/.

About the Author – Sam Miner

I am a junior at the University of St. Thomas studying Communication and Journalism alongside Justice and Peace Studies. I am passionate about media and the different outlets and variations that it can encompass. I am also the opinions editor for TommieMedia, an outlet I utilize to formulate and share my written opinions. After I graduate I hope to continue my passion for producing media in whatever form that make take, with hopeful emphasis on a paying job.

Minnesota Coalition for the Homeless
Henry Ripple

Story

In 2009, a study of key findings of homelessness in Minnesota was published. Comprised of countless interviews and observations about the issue of homelessness, the results were rather shocking. People living without homes find themselves confronted with difficulties never experienced. Awful circumstances and lack of support from the government guided their lives to be on the streets and/or struggling to find someone who has room for them to sleep in the cold of a night. Tyrell is an eighteen-year-old male who spends nights on the streets and at his sister's house when he can. Difficult home life led to his life without a roof over his head. Violence and abuse within his family led to his mom kicking him out of the house and forcing him to spend his nights wondering where he could sleep that night. It's hard for him to even find a shelter for the homeless or to find any kind of employment so that he may have a chance at some form of comfort. At the very least, the comfort of not sleeping on the cold ground. He wants to be a musician and has some talented singing and rapping skills, but because the resources are not there, it will be hard for him. Shawna is a forty-year-old woman who also lived a life without the comfort of a bed. She was born to a mother and father who got divorced when she was only six months old. She spent her early childhood living with her mom. Her mother was a neglectful parent who suffered from alcoholism. It was not a safe place for a child to be raised. When Shawna was 8 years old, her circumstances got even worse. Her mother brought her to Arizona and left her there alone. She struggled for a long time, trying to piece together why her mother had done this and began blaming herself. Eventually, Shawna had children, but she began to suffer the same problems of alcohol addiction that her mother had. In a way, she saw herself become more and more like her mother had been. Eventually, her children were taken away and she was without a home, living on the streets. It took a lot of strength and support, but she finally overcame addiction and kicked alcohol so that she could be sober when she sees her grandchildren for the first time. As of 2009, findings show that approximately 13,100 Minnesotans on any night are living without homes. From a large group of 9,654 people who are homeless: 23% are females that are 22 years or older, 30% are males that are 22 or older, 34% are children with their parents, 11% are unaccompanied young adults that are 18-22, and 2% are unaccompanied minors. These statistics show that around half of people without homes that were counted are children and young adults. Studies also showed a trend of exponential increase over previous years. In 1991, an estimate of 3,500 people lived without homes. Over the next couple years, a few thousand more would be included that number, and in 2009 that number rose to an estimated 13,100 people living without homes. An increase of 10,000 in people that can't sleep in a bed. This was a clear issue in Minnesota. (Wilder Research)

The Minnesota Coalition for the Homeless was energized with a fuel from sadness and anger that so many of their fellow Minnesotans had nowhere to go at the end of the day. Most of them didn't even have a place to go during the day because of their lack of employment. Not due to their personalities, but because their circumstances and lack of support created these awful challenges. It was 2003 when the Minnesota Coalition for the Homeless realized that they needed to officially add position statements that would guide their mission and keep their focus on the issues they believed were their duty to be a support system for. The first is human rights and the belief that housing falls under the category of a basic human right. This means that my subject would strive to oppose all legislation and policies that would diminish this basic human right. Their 2nd statement is Housing and working with service providers, housing developers and cities to construct and preserve safe and quality housing that is affordable for low and very low-income Minnesotans. The 3rd statement is Income Security and the notion that homelessness and poverty are directly linked. They believe the government must push forward in making sure everyone can get an income that allows them to afford housing, food, and healthcare. Their 4th statement is Intervention, Prevention, and Outreach, which calls on all to work with them to help "prevent or mitigate homelessness…by participation in systemic change initiatives and by making housing an integral part of client discharge planning." Health Security is another one of their statements that promotes a knowledgeable understanding of the difficulty of access to health care and what must be done to change that, so health care can be accessible for more people. Their final statement is Professionalization of Services, which strives for an always improving understanding of homelessness and an increase in quality and outcomes with "funders, legislators, service providers, and homeless people." The Minnesota Coalition for the Homeless made a few staggering achievements as direct outcomes from their decisions to provide strict and active focus on striving to solve homelessness and the issues that allow homelessness to be possible. One of their larger achievements was the outcome of many campaigns and strategic movements that pushed for a piece of legislation to be passed. The successful piece of legislation that came about would guarantee $100 million in bonds that would directly go to constructing and preserving houses across Minnesota. It allowed 5,000 housing units for homeless people in MN to be built and maintained. My subject also coordinates two additional outcomes that would demonstrate their understanding of issues that lead to homelessness. One of which was a bill that would allow parents who participate in the Minnesota Family Investment Program to be eligible for unlimited access and participation in adult basic education. This allowed 60% of parents enrolled to receive their GED and the other 40% to receive post-secondary training and education. It is important to note that among the massive issue of homelessness, these are only minor steps, but it is these steps that allow more and more acceleration towards tearing down the pillars that cause homelessness. (Minnesota Coalition for the Homeless)

Theory

The concept I chose that is embodied by the Minnesota Coalition for the Homeless is democratizing leadership. "A collaborative leadership team and participatory structure…enhanced individual and collective agency by giving delegates regular opportunities to use voice together, structured consensus decision making processes, and opportunities to engage in collective action" (Klein 26). Through numerous examples, this organization has demonstrated that it has a full understanding of the meaning of this concept and how to successfully carry out actions that promote a democratic leadership. Their distribution of power within the organization, their collective actions shared with local individuals and organizations, and their mission prove that they act without a singular power and instead promote communication and action developed with large amounts of people who share their beliefs.

One of their proud achievements is acting as a hub for organizations and individuals in different areas who share their mission of working to end homelessness. Instead of recruiting these people and garnering a large following to increase the size of the organization, they offer their service through connect people to communicate and share ideas to follow through on a collective mission. This has been a focus of the organization since the beginning, in 1984. They now serve as a hub for communication and shared knowledge with around 150 different organizations, along with more individuals who are passionate about the issue and want to work together to reach an end to homelessness.

118

The local power within the organization is another example of how they have a deep belief in a democratic leadership. They have many directors who each tackle a small, detailed issue and focus on researching and understanding more about the issue and the factors that are causing it. This allows them to have a dialogue with one another and share their knowledge so that, as a collective group, they can to communicate different tactics for dealing with the issue. Oftentimes this leads them to reach to others in the community to discuss the issue and how to act. They want the community to know that they have just as much impact on the tactics. The mission statement of the organization is as follows, "The mission of the Minnesota Coalition for the Homeless is to generate policies, community support and local resources for housing and services to end homelessness in Minnesota." They provide a clear and concise explanation of what they want to do and how they believe in utilizing the community to work with them to help solve the issue. They often look for support in local, community-based organizations that have the resources to combat homelessness. (Minnesota Coalition for the Homeless)

Democratizing leadership eliminates singular control over an organization. It eliminates the danger of allowing corruption to take charge as it takes that power and voice and equally spreads to all who choose to be heard. At a time in history where a leader of a nation is ignoring the cries and needs of its people and only focuses on ruling with self-gain in mind, democratizing leadership is a ray of hope in an otherwise gloomy period. It can upset the establishment and yield power to the people who deserve to have a say in how matters are conducted. Now, more than ever, the people need to be heard. So many voices are silenced by the deafening actions of a power-hungry man and it is important to usher in change through a unification of the people and stand up to the anti-democratic leadership that is running rampant.

Action Plan

My personal action plan will be to gather people across the Twin Cities with each other so that their voices can be heard and understood. I want to create a sense of unity that will guide our movements progressions through a series of demonstrations that will influence external threats of the perspectives they have not considered. As challenging and harrowing as it will be, I am confident that the people who join my group are up to the challenge. They have seen and experienced every external threat I can imagine, and their strength of knowledge and passion will give us the upper hand to a successful movement.

I would begin my personal action plan, theorizing ways to utilize the strength I have observed and in what ways these strengths could progress my action plan closer to the ultimate end goal: provide all Twin Cities residents with affordable housing. Our strength comes in the numbers of passionate people who have suffered lives without roofs over their head and are fueled by a willingness to provide better for their future generations and themselves. That is why the first step in my plan is forming a connection between these people in the Twin Cities. A good place to start would be flyers and posters everywhere that is occupied by those living without homes. I want these posters to inform them that this is their movement and not some form of charity from me and other people who have comfortable living situations. They are the ones whose voices will be the most powerful. These posters need to let them know when and where we can all meet and simply introduce and each other and share stories of the unfair circumstances they have been brought up in. Their strength in numbers and in passion will guide the action plan through the next steps.

It will be important to address our weakness. This will not be a day and night change. This will be a grueling, lengthy movement that may be tiny steps forward and unfortunate steps backward throughout the process. We will need to make this obvious from the get-go so as not to be blinded by false hope that everything will work perfectly in a short amount of time. That is why this step is another crucial issue that will need to be addressed. We will begin with where we are now and what the ultimate end goal is. This will help us remember why it is we are doing what we are doing when we are hit with extreme hardships. For example, let's say a massive piece of legislation is going to be voted on that will transition huge sums of money to be used for affordable housing construction and to construct organizations of support for those living without homes. It will be a monumental achievement for us and will save thousands of lives from cold and wet nights of sleep. We have endured months of hardcore, grueling advocating and some of us have even been locked up in the county jails, even though all of our demonstrations have been absolutely peaceful. Well, the results just came in and the legislation was tossed aside by a mere single vote. It would be so easy for us to give up at the hands of this gut-wrenching blow, but our vision of the perfect end goal will remind us why it is that we started this movement in the first place.

I believe another extremely important part of our plan will be internal support for each other within the movement. These people who have decided to become a part of the change are risking a lot to help not only themselves but all of those around them. This sense of unity is our opportunity at persevering what most people would have quit after suffering defeats like the previous example that was just mentioned. A plan to promote this opportunity is to have consistent meetings that will not even deal with strategic action planning but will be focused on strengthening our unity. Support groups, round-table discussions, and shared meals every week are a few things that could be done to continue strengthening our movement's dynamics with one another. It will remind us all that we are not doing it for ourselves so much as all of those around us. I think that this step in our movement's action is just as important if not more so than the active steps taken to host demonstrations around the Twin Cities. I believe at every stage of the movement's plan, making sure that we always have a place to go back to and remind each other that we are still humans with issues and loneliness and that we will always have a sense of unity with each other.

This previous step in our movement's progression will ultimately help with the issue of internal threats. We will all know each other personally and will have formed a unity with one another. If an outsider attempts to thwart our attempts through internal spying, pretending to be one of our members, we will find out one way or another. Our weekly meetings that are built upon openness and sharing will help us all understand each other and will also help us recognize an imposter or someone who is lying about their difficulties or honesties. Now, external threats will come in all shapes and all sizes at every stage of the movement and even after the movement may end in the future. The important thing to remember is the original step of the entire plan. Envisioning the perfect difference that we could instill in the world and even though it is improbable to be totally completed in our lifetime, the very idea of this dream goal being achieved is possible. We have accepted the external threats because our members have lived with external threats all their life. They have been trained by their awful circumstances that there will always be external threats. Yet, the important thing to remember in these times is to remember why we refuse to believe hatred as a proper response. We have seen the possible happiness that unity can bring within our own movement and we know that that is something worth spreading. Even if many external parties seem extremely opposed to receiving our helping hand.

It will be hard, improbable even, but as I've read up on some of the most famous peaceful movements in history, I know that it was never easy for them. Dr. King and his fellow advocates took beatings and terroristic violence from hate-filled people and yet progressed. Even if they wavered, they were unified by their voices and their passion that they knew would demonstrate their willingness to never stop pushing our cause on every external threat to them. I want my action plan to revolve around unity and passion. These will be the strengths of the movement and will guide us when the odds are absolutely stacked against the movement. It won't matter if our group' voices are always heard and supported by one another.

About the Author - Henry Ripple

I grew up in Chanhassen, Minnesota and attended Montessori school through 8th grade. Teachers at the Montessori school were early influences on Social Justice becoming a passion. Currently, en route to receive a degree in Justice and Peace Studies, I look forward to opportunities to serve my fellow people.

Works Cited

Minnesota Coalition for the Homeless. (n.d.). Retrieved December 18, 2017, from https://www.mnhomelesscoalition.org/

Shelton, E. (2010, May). Homelessness in Minnesota. Retrieved December 19, 2017, from http://www.wilder.org/Wilder-Research/Publications/Studies/Homelessness%20in%20Minnesota,%202009%20Study/Homelessness%20in%20Minnesota%20-%20Key%20Findings,%20Summary.pdf

Minnesota Literacy Council
Carly Steinauer

Story

      Each year, the Minnesota Literacy Council publishes an anthology of adult student writing titled *Journeys*. This anthology offers the perspectives of Minnesota adult literacy students enrolled in reading, English as a Second Language (ESL or ELL for short), GED, and basic skills classes across the state (Journeys, 2013). These students are diverse in nationality, culture, language, and circumstance. *Journeys* aims to provide a space for students to tell their own stories in their own words, and an opportunity for others to listen. They speak of memories, friendships, interests, struggles, families, cultures, and goals. They are stories that come from snowy cabins in Minnesota, Ramadan feasts around an Ethiopian dinner table, and Burmese villages surrounded by mountains, rivers and trees. Each of these stories connect us to one another. They provide adult literacy students with an opportunity to read and learn stories that reflect people like themselves, and they provide a glimpse into the lives of people similar and different to us in ways that reflect our common humanity. One of these stories from the 2013 edition of Journeys tells one woman's story about her adjustment to the United States.

      Nhu* (name has been changed to protect identity) was forty-seven years old when she relocated to a country nearly 9,000 miles and an ocean away. For forty-seven years, Nhu called Vietnam home. In 1975, the communist government in North Vietnam took over South Vietnam. Her husband, a military officer in the Republic Government, was jailed for seven years in a Communist prison. As reparation, Nhu and her family were offered refugee status in America in 1997. Nhu remembers how she felt upon her arrival in the United States. "I felt that I was dumb, deaf and blind. I couldn't hear and understand English. I was very miserable." Nhu and her husband began to go to ELL classes. During this time, they had to juggle school and work. Nhu remembers waiting for the bus in the cold winter weather and working long hours, from 3:30 pm to midnight. She continued to study and learn English through classes and conversations with American co-workers. Nhu writes that it is her dream to improve her English as she continues her life in the United States (Journeys, 2013).

The mission of the Minnesota Literacy Council is to share the power of learning through education, community building, and advocacy. In a sense, their goal is to work to replace feelings of deafness and blindness with agency and empowerment. MLC's extensive volunteer network lends itself to stronger community building within the state. Janet Curiel, a long time ESL teacher within this network, has seen strengthening of community take root in her classroom. Janet lives and works in the Cedar Riverside community of Minneapolis, where a majority of her students are immigrants and refugees from Eastern Africa. Janet, having experienced relocation herself, understands some of the challenges associated with trying to learn a new language in a new country. She has seen many students that come through her classroom experience difficulties like the ones Nhu faced when relocating to the United States. While Janet knows ESL classes are very important to new immigrants who do not speak the language, she also notes the burden it places on her students. Many of her students are young women responsible for caring for children and the household while working as much as possible to provide for their families in the United States or back in their country of origin. Like

Nhu, many of her students attend class in the mornings before they work long hours late into the night. Janet knows there is an ache for home and family that drives her students. When volunteers come into her classroom, Janet recognizes the agency they possess as English speakers. Many of these volunteers are university students. As such, Janet believes they have a greater capacity to advocate for the ESL students they work with. Many have gone on to work with refugee organizations, the Peace Corps, or have ended up becoming ESL teachers themselves. Janet believes all volunteers in her classroom take their experiences with them and are generally more open and understanding of immigrant and refugee populations (J. Curiel, personal communication, October 27, 2017).

Both Nhu and Janet Curiel's experiences with adult education are centered largely around immigrant and refugee populations in ELL classes. While supporting and advocating for these students, volunteers, and programs is a large part of the Minnesota Literacy Council's work, there are also other kinds of students and programs involved in the mission. Eric Nesheim, the executive director of the Minnesota Literacy Council, notes that the definition of literacy is changing. Rather than just an ability to read and write, MLC is expanding their view of literacy to include things like ESL, citizenship, workforce skills, GED and basic skills, and technology. Eric views literacy as essential in providing people with the agency to work, understand things like transportation and healthcare, and provide educational aid for their children. Based on this expanded view of literacy, the Minnesota Literacy Council believes roughly one in ten people in the state of Minnesota is functionally illiterate. While between 70,000 and 80,000 people each year come through literacy programs throughout the state, Eric Nesheim and the MLC believe this is only a small portion of those struggling with literacy in the state. Eric believes this may be because people are busy working to provide for themselves and their families, or do not want to admit they struggle with literacy (E. Nesheim, personal communication, 2017). These people may be native Minnesotans, immigrants, refugees, or United States citizens. The

Minnesota Literacy Council recognizes the existing need for literacy education in the state and continues to use education, community building, and advocacy to expand its reach to ensure everyone in the state has access to agency building education.

Theory

No social movement, idea, problem or solution occurs in a vacuum. Rather, they are shaped by the context in which they exist and must be navigated as such. In his book, *The Moral Imagination*, John Paul Lederach outlines the importance of this concept as he describes his theory of the web of relationships. Nothing in the world exists in isolation; the same is true for social problems and organizations. It is necessary, then, to analyze the web of relationships when considering how to address a problem or work towards a goal. Lederach articulates that cycles of violence are broken when individuals and communities are able to imagine themselves in a web of relationship even with their enemies (Lederach 2005 p. 34). Understanding and using this web is key; positive change cannot occur without interdependency. Lederach conceptualizes this theory through his work in conflict resolution in Central America where he learned to not only consider solutions, but people. "When people in everyday settings where I was working had a conflict, their first thought was not 'what is the solution?' It was 'who do I know who knows the person with whom I have the problem who can help create a way out?'" (Lederach 2005 p. 77). Lederach learned to consider relationships as central to conflict transformation. He states, "to put it another way, solutions emerged from relational resources, connections, and obligations," (Lederach 2005 p. 77). The Minnesota Literacy Council describes its history as such: A group of women realized if one person taught someone to read, and that person taught someone to read, they could create a movement. They knew early on that literacy is critical to growth and self-sufficiency, planting the seed for reading programs and statewide volunteer training (Minnesota Literacy Council). Illiteracy does not occur on its own; it exists within a context of literacy. In this way, the

MLC uses relationships to transform issues around literacy in the state. In 2010 alone, the Minnesota Literacy Council trained more than 2,500 individuals to be adult literacy tutors and directly placed 550 of those volunteers in literacy programs throughout the state (Minnesota Literacy Council). Through these interpersonal interactions with volunteers, the MLC does not only ask what the solution is to addressing literacy within the state; they ask who needs to be a part of the process.

The Minnesota Literacy Council also works on an organizational level to help strengthen and support other literacy programs throughout the state. One example of this comes from a neighborhood in Minneapolis. In 2011, the Lyndale Neighborhood Association estimated that there were over 6,000 residents in the neighborhood who spoke a language other than English at home and sought to create an ESL program to address resident's needs. After conducting an initial review to ensure services were not being duplicated, the Minnesota Literacy Council worked with the Lyndale Neighborhood Association to create a sustainable volunteer-led ESL program model. MLC provided teacher training and volunteer placement, and within the first three months, the program had thirty ESL students (Minnesota Literacy Council). If the relationship between the Lyndale Neighborhood Association and the Minnesota Literacy Council did not exist, MLC would not have known to address the need where it existed, and the residents of Lyndale neighborhood may not have received the services they needed.

The Minnesota Literacy Council uses relationships between organizations to promote literacy, but they also focus on interpersonal relationship building and advocacy to advance their mission. John Paul Lederach uplifts this kind of relationship building when he speaks of the web of relationships in leadership. He says, "Breaking violence requires that people embrace a more fundamental truth: Who we have been, are, and will be emerges and shapes itself in a context of relational interdependency," (Lederach 2005 p. 35). Janet Curiel, a long time ESL teacher in the Cedar Riverside community of Minneapolis, speaks to the importance of interpersonal relationships between literacy learners and volunteers. When asked about the volunteers who come through her classroom, Janet said, "We do want them to be aware and sensitive and understanding and working, not just to come here for the experience but also to hopefully be thinking of ways to equalize things more," (J. Curiel, personal communication, October 27, 2017). Not only can these relationships between students and volunteers foster greater interpersonal understanding and mutuality, Janet has seen these relationships take form through advocacy. The Minnesota Literacy Council makes it part of their mission to advocate for literacy throughout the state. These interpersonal and organizational relationships aid in advocacy work. MLC works to advocate for increased funding for adult basic education throughout the state and encourages volunteers to share experiences with others in their communities as well as elected officials. This web of relationships can continue to strengthen literacy work throughout the state through both organizations and policy. Going forward, the importance of relationship building in areas of policy advocacy work specifically might be framed using Lederach's web of relationships. Not only might we consider what needs to be done, but who should be involved in the conversations. By building a larger web, the conversation may grow louder and longer.

Action Plan

The Minnesota Literacy Council employs a number of strategies to work towards the organization's vision and mission (Minnesota Literacy Council) . MLC's strategic plan outlines this mission: to share the power of learning through education, community building, and advocacy. This plan provides the organization with strategic direction specifically from 2015 to 2018, leaving room for evaluation and improvement in the future. The strategies focus largely on advocacy and visibility, diversity and inclusion, and partnerships and collaboration. Through the lens of advocacy and visibility, the Minnesota Literacy Council asks how it might shed light on issues around literacy, both locally and internationally. Part of this strategy works to define and create greater visibility for literacy learners-- a category that continues to change as education in communities change. Literacy learners today might include people like Nhu, who use English Language Learner programs to help navigate an unfamiliar country, or someone who is struggling with technology in an electronic age.

The strategic lens of diversity and inclusion works to ensure literacy services are effective and representative in the communities in which they operate. MLC's focus on partnership and collaboration employs Lederach's web of relationships to ensure the cause of literacy in Minnesota (Lederach 2005). This focus enables collaboration between literacy organizations to reach more literacy learners and improve existing programs (Minnesota Literacy Council).

All three of these strategic lenses have roots in the social change wheel, a diagram that considers various strategies to achieve social change. The wheel maps out various arenas in which progressive change might occur. At the center of the wheel: education. Subsequent areas of the social change wheel include formal political processes, direct service, community building, capacity building, grassroots organizing, and confrontational strategies. Each of these arenas provide a unique strategy for realizing a mission rooted in social change. The Minnesota Literacy Council's vision of literate communities is advanced through their strategic lenses listed earlier, each of which correspond to several aspects of the social change wheel. Education is the main strategy of MLC in that it is used to aid those who struggle with literacy. However, education could also take form not only teacher to student, but volunteer to those in his or her web of relationships. Education could be a direct service, or a form of advocacy to increase visibility for the cause of literacy. MLC's strategic lens of partnership and collaboration takes form through the sharing of education between organizations to create better literacy programs. Subsequently, community building utilizes MLC's web of relationships. These relationships are built between student and teacher, or volunteers from various backgrounds who work to create an inclusive environment and foster relationships between different communities. MLC's strategic lens of diversity and inclusion falls into this category of social change strategy. Finally, advocacy and visibility are realized largely through formal political processes. MLC continues to lobby the state of Minnesota for increased funding for literacy programs for organizations throughout the state, as the resources granted by these funds enable Minnesota to continue to have some of the highest rates of literacy in the country ("State and County Estimates of Low Literacy." 2003).

While these are some of the primary strategies used by the Minnesota Literacy Council, there are some areas of the social change wheel that are not as prevalent in the organization's strategies, namely grassroots organizing and confrontational strategies. Most of MLC's leadership and organization comes from the top down. Eric Nesheim, executive director of the Minnesota Literacy Council noted that while collaboration is important to the organization, most decision making ultimately lies with board members and the executive director (Nesheim 2017).

There is a balance to be struck between formalization and collaboration and participation. This kind of hierarchical model of decision-making certainly has its benefits, but perhaps this compromise loses some benefits of more grassroots models of leadership (Klein, 2017). Further, confrontational strategies can often be an important way in which movements for social change increase momentum and awareness. While tactics like these are not employed by the Minnesota Literacy Council, the importance of visibility to the cause of literacy is not lost on the organization. Again, there lies a tension between improvisation and formalization in a more structured organization like the Minnesota Literacy Council.

Not all strategies of the social change wheel are used by the Minnesota Literacy Council. While the organization relies on the use of education and community building, it overlooks areas like grassroots organizing and confrontational strategies. However, one of the core strategies outlined by the organization is its commitment to partnership and collaboration with other literacy minded groups. Perhaps some of these groups around the state tend to focus on more grassroots leadership and organizing, offering a different perspective. MLC's strategic plan from 2015-2018 notes that other literacy organizations may benefit from MLC's expertise in the field. Perhaps this notion could be broadened to consider what other literacy organizations could share with them, from leadership styles to program visibility and what lies in between. Another strength of this strategic plan lies in its expiration date. In 2018, this plan will be reconsidered to evaluate which strategies worked, and which did not. Good leadership considers its mission and understands that there is always room to learn. The goal of literacy is enormous, and good leadership is paramount to its realization.

Works Cited

Journeys: An Anthology of Adult Student Writing. (2013). Saint Paul, MN: Minnesota Literacy Council.

Klein, M. (2017). Creative Tensions in Social Movement Organizations (SMOs), unpublished manuscript, used with permission.

Lederach, J. P. (2005). *The Moral Imagination: the Art and Soul of Building Peace.* New York, NY: Oxford University Press.

Minnesota Literacy Council. (n.d.). Retrieved November 21, 2017, from https://mnliteracy.org/

"State and County Estimates of Low Literacy." State and County Literacy Estimates – State Estimates, National Center for Education Statistics, 2003, https://nces.ed.gov/naal/estimates/StateEstimates.aspx

About the Author – Carly Steinauer

I am a senior at the University of St. Thomas studying Political Science and Justice and Peace Studies, where I have learned to critically evaluate the reality of the world with which I have been presented. My hobbies include listening to podcasts, being an ESL classroom assistant at Cedar Riverside Adult Education Collaborative, and drawing Orca whales.

Minnesota Public Interest Research Group
Hazel Erickson

Story

Forty-six years ago, in the midst of the Vietnam War, activism and organizing on campuses around the nation spread like wildfire. Of course, Minnesota also felt the heat of political activism. Students at the University of Minnesota-Twin Cities needed a voice. So, in 1971, over fifty percent of the student body signed a petition to charge themselves a fee (at the time it was only about $1) to hire staff, lawyers, and lobbyists just like big businesses could. The fee immediately went to lawyers and researchers who looked into state politics and what could be done on behalf of students in Minnesota. Thus, began Minnesota Public Interest Research Group, or MPIRG, and its advocacy by and for the students.

MPIRG members - all students - elect an executive board to run the organization and hire staff. Top staff includes an organizing director and campus organizer. Every year, there is a large-initiatives meeting is held where new goals are set and ideas are suggested. Every three years, standing platform issues are cycled out and new issues are chosen. The current cycle is focused on economic, environmental, and racial justice. MPIRG educates their members on these issues and teaches them how to effectively advocate. Of course, tactics are not limited to protest. Phone banks, door knocking, speaking to classes, social media, letters to the editor, and general peer to peer conversation are all ways encouraged and supported at MPIRG. Overall, the goal of MPIRG is not just to create social change in communities across the state of Minnesota, it is to create the next generation of politically active young adults. Ian Kantonen, Organizing Director, put it perfectly when he referred to MPIRG as, "a leadership development pipeline that creates engaged citizens." America needs engaged citizens. MPIRG works to create and foster leaders in communities and government. Students on the executive board, who mentor and support the next executive board, gain knowledge on how to effectively educate others and themselves not only on the issues. They also work towards and accomplish solutions to such issues.

  MPIRG has a legacy of accomplishments. Starting in 1978, the Boundary Waters Canoe Area Wilderness Act passed and created the nation's only exclusively paddle-zone wilderness area. By the eighties, MPIRG had around twenty chapters at schools all over Minnesota and Public Interest Research Groups all around the nation were getting attention. Unfortunately, that wave of activism passed and Minnesota State Colleges and Universities (MNSCU) made rules which cut student fees and blocked fees to organizations such as MPIRG. So, as MPIRG could not pay staff to keep their posts at every college, chapters began to blink out across the state. Meanwhile, the work continued. In 1990, MPIRG advocated to ban the dumping of "low level" radioactive waste from landfills and incinerators. Not only that, but states around the nation used MPIRG's legislation and research as models for their state's legislation. In the long term, federal policy concerning similar legislation was reversed, thus extending MPIRG's influence to a national level as they helped swing the national interest and argument. In 1998, MPIRG lobbied for the metro greenways and natural areas project. In the end, about 4 million dollars of funding were allocated to protect and restore important ecological areas while accommodating urban growth.

In 2008, MPIRG ran a massive campaign to help register students to vote and eventually gained about 15,000-20,000 young voters. Again in 2012, MPIRG worked to mobilize the youth vote and significantly altered the outcome of the "vote no" amendments that year. Evidence shows that campuses with active MPIRG chapters were more likely to vote no on the constitutional ban on marriage equality and an amendment to restrict voting rights.

Recently, MPIRG has been working with students to help speak out against Line 3, the oil pipeline scheduled to cut through the northern part of the state, in addition to getting students out to vote in local and national elections, and the lowering of student debt.

Minnesota Public Interest Research Group has no doubt made a lasting impact on communities across the state and has accomplished impressive goals over the years, but most important is the impact they created on the people. MPIRG has been creating generations of active students that learn how to educate others and create real change within communities. Students involved contribute and work towards excellent causes, not only build a strong community, but a strong sense of self as well.

Theory

"I'm sorry, can you repeat that?" I asked incredulously, eyes wide, as I squirmed in my seat. I walked into this interview completely cold, painfully nervous, and completely oblivious to what I had within my grasp. Ian Kantonen, Organizing Director for MPIRG, looked back at me with a smile, "When can you start?"

I was halfway through my first year of college and even the deep freeze of February couldn't subdue the fire that sparked within me from the 2016 election cycle. I wanted to get involved but didn't know how. A friend from the University of Minnesota briefly mentioned MPIRG and gave me Ian's email, but I was incredibly unsure. Could I join so far into the school year? What could I, a fledgling freshman, contribute? Even if I could contribute, how much with my busy school schedule? All my concerns disappeared after my interview with Ian. MPIRG (and Ian) gave me the opportunity not only to get involved with the political process in the Twin Cities, but provided me with the education I needed to do so. Thus, the theory of community organizing at MPIRG is applied not only through the organizing they do themselves, but (perhaps more importantly) through their work to educate youth on community organizing.

An important foundation to community organizing is to identify issues and create goals. The student leaders of MPIRG and the Directors they hire are aware of this, as any group without defined and achievable goals will struggle to create any lasting or meaningful change. So, at the beginning of each school year, students gather in MPIRG headquarters on University Avenue in Minneapolis to discuss and vote on the three standing platforms of the year. Here, one of the three is scrapped, redefined, or even replaced. This year, the three platforms are Economic Justice, Environmental Justice, and Racial Justice. After these are established, students identify key issues within each platform and create smaller and more focused campaigns with feasible goals. For example, fighting for environmental justice by speaking against oil pipeline "Line 3" at community hearings, working to restore the vote for past felons (who are disproportionately people of color) for racial justice by holding workshops on how to lobby lawmakers, and holding informational meetings about the implementation of a $15 minimum wage so then students can educate others on the economic justice of a higher minimum wage. MPIRG chapters across Minnesota are free to tackle these issues under the standing platforms in any way they wish. With this in mind, rural chapters tend to be more environmentally focused while the more urban chapters tend to work more on economic and racial justice.

Moreover, leaders within each chapter work to educate their members on these issues and how to properly and effectively take action against them. For instance, when I interned for MPIRG in the spring of 2017 at the Minnesota State Capitol, Ian gave me a tour of all the buildings on Capitol Hill, showed me the committee hearing rooms, explained committee procedure, *et cetera.* I sat in on the Environment and Natural Resources Policy and Finance House Committee, took notes, and filled out a form reporting any legislation that could be potentially harmful to the environment. This is just one example of the work MPIRG does to not only organize students, but to teach them as well.

Conclusively, MPIRG is not just a community organizer alone. It is also a structured and effective organization which instructs and develops youth in community organizing so that they may take that knowledge and apply it to their lives after their time with the organization. In a way, MPIRG is a double-edged sword fighting social injustice by building meaningful organizations with motivated young people who do more than what they set out to accomplish within the organization. They also go on to use the skills they acquire in their own communities and lives. This is the greatest asset to communities, and to social justice in general, an organization can offer. Imagine if every community of young people had a chapter of MPIRG, or an organization which offers similar services, to educate and empower them. The benefits would not only be immediate, but increase over time as more and more people participate in community organizing is immeasurably valuable.

Action Planning

On the day before my nineteenth birthday and for the first time ever, I was certain I was the first girl awake in my dorm. I climbed down the ladder of my bunk bed and stumbled about my room in the dark, obsessing over which blazer to choose and which heels would be appropriate. By six-thirty, I was huddled at a bus stop near campus, watching the sun slowly spread across the snow. By seven-thirty, I had already transferred from bus to train to coffee cart and, steamy drink and folder in hand, I sat on a cool marble bench in the basement of the State Capitol.

There, among old pillars and portraits, I softly rehearsed my testimony, picking at details, making last-minute scrawls and scratches.

The night before, I had poured over the facts of the Student Loan Tax Credit Bill about to be brought through the Minnesota Senate and House Tax Committees with the help of MPIRG's Ian Kantonen, as he spent much time emailing and texting me details, explanations, and plans. I was ready.

The rest of the day was a blur. When I was called to speak I was eager, earnest, and most importantly: *empowered*. This was not a cookie-cutter speech. MPIRG coached me on committee rules, provided me with materials concerning the bill, and advised me on the language of my testimony but the words, the belief, and the passion were all mine. Because of MPIRG, I learned how to successfully testify for a bill I supported.

Of course, MPIRG does much more than this. Their most important strategy on the Social Change Wheel is Education. MPIRG builds from this segment of the Social Change Wheel and applies it to all the other segments: Grassroots Organizing, Community Building, Formal Political Process, Confrontational Strategies, Direct Service, and Capacity Building.

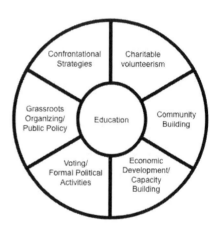

MPIRG's Grassroots Organizing does more than educate students on how to testify. They also host lobbying days at the state capitol. One I attended, which was in support of affirmative consent legislation: a bill to ensure schools implement programs to teach students on consent and the presence of an explicit, voluntary, informed, and continual 'yes' in regards of sexual activity.

Additionally, they have hosted door-knocking and phone bank teach-ins to educate the community on matters pertinent to them and to students. MPIRG also promotes Community Organizing. For example, in December of 2017, MPIRG called for students and campus communities to stand with University of Minnesota workers in their strike for better wages. Formal Political Process at MPIRG is a little tricky because they are a non-profit, but MPIRG has hosted massive get-out-to-vote initiatives and voter registration events to ensure political activity in students and local communities. Confrontational Strategies vary but include: sitting in the Chancellor's office, marches, and picketing. Direct Service includes events such as biking safety in the winter and informational teach-ins on the rights of students as tenants and how to deal with landlords. Finally, Capacity Building is also a solid foundation at MPIRG along with Education, as all the work MPIRG and its members do is to build people's capacity to create a better, more just world.

Works Cited

MPIRG. Retrieved from http://mpirg.org

About the Author – Hazel Erickson

I will be graduating from the University of Saint Thomas in May of 2020 with a triple major in Political Science, Communication and Journalism, and Justice and Peace Studies. When I'm not in class, you can catch me singing in UST's Concert Choir, at an Undergraduate Student Government Meeting, tweeting for the UST College Democrats, or co-writing The Activist Digest with Cari Monroe. My favorite pastimes include spending time with friends and loved ones, reading classic books, and keeping up with local and national politics. I'd like to thank my mother, Sarah Erickson, and my grandparents, Jerry and Kathleen Erickson, for their continual love, support, and positive influence. They are the spark that ignited my passion for social justice.

Sexual Violence Center
Sidney Severson

Story

On a particularly brisk Thursday afternoon in October, I paid a visit to the SVC, located at 2021 East Hennepin Avenue, in Minneapolis. On this visit, I was due to meet with Sarah Borger, who is the program director at the SVC. The purpose of my visit was to learn more about the center, gather information beyond that their website could offer me, ask questions about their mission, and the work they conduct on a daily basis at SVC.

I chose the Sexual Violence Center for my project, simply because sexual violence, against anyone, women in particular, is something that I have always been passionate about. This comes from the anger I have about the ways that women are disproportionately affected by this type of violence, and the way victims are treated. I have been drawn to this particular area of injustice, also largely because I am a woman, and have grown to be hyper-aware of the dangers that exist in my life because of that. And, because I know way too many women who have experienced sexual violence. The Sexual Violence Center felt like a good pick for me because they are doing the work I hope to be involved in some day.

Instead of telling the story of one individual, and their experience at The Sexual Violence Center, I am going to focus on the wide range of people the center not only attracts, but welcomes. Each case, and person that The Sexual Violence Center deals with is unique. The victims are unique in the way they cope, and also unique in how close they are to being able to advocate for themselves and call themselves not just victims, but survivors. The Sexual Violence Center got their start by splitting off from a larger agency, but felt that sexual violence work was something of importance that they considered a "stand-alone issue" in Sarah's words. From there, they moved into their first space, which they actually just moved out of less than one month prior to my meeting with Sarah. When I arrived for my meeting, I was so warmly welcomed by Sarah as well as several other members of the staff, and into her new office, that she was still settling into. She gave me a tour of the space, and explained what the rooms were designated for, and would look like after they were completed. She also explained the several reasons that The Sexual Violence Center had moved from the house it had previously operated in, to the office building where it is now found. She cited reasons as simple as outgrowing the space, but others like the benefits of moving closer to the city, being more accessible to people, and public transportation routes, as well as the fact that because so many businesses operate out of their new building, the people who are seeking out their services are much less exposed because it is not at all obvious where they might be going. All of these things are extremely important to the employees at the Sexual Violence Center, as they are wholeheartedly committed to eradicating sexual violence, and anything they can do to make themselves more accessible, as well as making their patrons feel more comfortable.

The Sexual Violence Center offers a variety of different services, ranging from their twenty-four-hour crisis line, that victims can call, to group therapy sessions, individual, in person counseling, crisis support at the hospital, legal advocacy, and much more. Because like in this quote from their website highlights: "At the Sexual Violence Center, all of our services are provided by sexual assault advocates. The role of an advocate is to provide information, offer options and support victims and survivors in their decisions. It is up to you to determine which paths are best to take. You are your own best expert. You possess the power to define your own healing process. The advocate is in the role of facilitator. By sharing knowledge, giving choices, and acting as a liaison to various points in the system, our advocates are here to empower you." As is obvious in this statement, the primary concern of SVC is uplifting, and empowering their clients, and giving them as much control over their paths as they feel comfortable taking. They operate around meeting clients where they're at, and doing whatever possible to aid in helping their clients gain independence from their services.

What I love so much about this organization, and one of the main reasons that I was so drawn to it for this project, was that they work to eliminate any and all boundaries that could potentially keep their services from someone who needs them. I adore the undying and unconditional support the employees at the sexual violence center aim to give their clients, regardless of any circumstances that may present obstacles or challenges in their advocacy for any given client.

Theory

Sexual Violence does not see race, it does not see ethnicity, it does not see gender, nor does it see class. It does not care what you wear, how you behave, where you are, or who you're with. I would be hard pressed to find a person who has not, or is not being affected by sexual violence directly or indirectly. Sexual violence knows no bounds. Because of this, I am going to reference John Paul Lederach's theory of the "Web of Relationships" (2005). Reason being, I think an analysis that acknowledges the interconnectedness of people on social justice issues such as this one is inherently valuable.

It is easy, and natural, for people who have not been directly victimized by any given type of injustice, to turn away, and wash their hands of any responsibility, because if they are not a perpetrator, or a victim, how could it possibly be their problem? I can't say I don't understand this, especially over issues of injustice as daunting as sexual violence. However, it is this way of thinking that is also extremely problematic, because, if it's not my problem, and it's not yours, then whose problem is it? Unfortunately, the answer to this question is likely the victim's problem. This is not to say that victims can't or shouldn't play an important role in advocating against sexual violence; if they're willing, they absolutely should, however I don't think leaving them with all the work is fair either.

I like the idea of the Web of Relationships, because it is a simple. If you think about what a spider web looks like, it is a series of silks, or strings, running from all different directions, crossing paths at the center. Lederach equates the crossing of these paths to the ways that we as people are all connected, or "crossed" in one way or another. I think this is an important way to look at the issue of sexual violence, because I often see victim survivors advocating for themselves, which is, of course, phenomenal. I also see a lot of women showing support for those victim/survivors, which again, is great, and although women are disproportionately affected by sexual violence, eradicating it is not only a women's issue.

The SVC is a fantastic resource for people who have been affected by sexual violence, and a fierce advocate for its eradication. Although they also educate on issues like consent as a preventative, they are often picking up the pieces, and helping people who have already been victimized. Of course, the work that is being done at SVC, is invaluable, but places like SVC alone, along with victim/survivors, are not the only people this injustice affects.

Every day, The Sexual Violence Center and their staff build meaningful relationships with their clients, they have relationships with other centers and organizations comparable to their own, as well as with local law enforcement, so that they can work better together, for these victims and against the issue of sexual violence.

Of course, the work of SVC is of utmost importance, but I think a really important question that we must ask ourselves is "how am I connected to this issue?" or, aligned with Lederach's analogy, what would my strand in the web around this issue be labeled? Advocate? Ally? Bystander? There is a place for all of us around this issue. The more we are aware of our current role- not only what we can do in helping to combat this injustice, the more we can challenge instead of uphold systems of power, control, and oppression. This is something that needs to happen in order to dismantle unjust systems and weave new webs based on justice.

I hope that this could encourage all of us to do some self-reflection, and challenge us to push ourselves to get more involved with this injustice, if we aren't already. We need to change our perception of the issue of sexual violence from a women's issue to an "us issue". What will you do to promote a healthy and more just web of relationships?

Action Plan

I chose The Sexual After researching the SVC for this project, and learning about the work they do, because I think that it is invaluable cause to work for because although women are disproportionately affected, no one is safe from the harmful effects of sexual violence. There are plenty of men who are affected by sexual violence, and I do not wish to discredit or invalidate them. In discussing this topic throughout this chapter, however I have geared my language largely towards women.

Sexual Violence against women has always been something I felt strongly about, however since coming to college, and declaring my major Justice and Peace Studies minor in Sociology, and getting to be involved in so many conversations around the issues of sexual violence, it has become more and more present in my mind, and in my priorities. It is likely that at some point in my career, I will find myself working directly on this issue. Even if I am not working in a job or at an organization that is centered around this social justice issue, I still want to learn, think about, and practice ways to be an advocate for victim/survivors regardless of where I find myself. Since I've been in college, and have had much more exposure to a diverse group of people, advocates, victims, survivors, and inspiration, around this issue, I have thought of myself as a sponge. I came in to St. Thomas, a farm girl from rural Wisconsin, without many people who were having, or wanted to have conversations about things that mattered. I found myself often dismissed. However, since being in college, and choosing the path that I have, I have found a multitude of people who have a fiery passion for social justice, eradicating sexual violence, and supporting those who have been victim survivors. I have found extremely diverse perspectives, opening my eyes to ways of viewing conversations, behaviors, policies, and the status quo that I did not previously know or see. I have found immense inspiration, many outlets, and learning opportunities in my professors, and my peers.

My personal goals after doing this project, are to challenge myself to find more ways to get involved, and to push myself out of my comfort zone. I want to explore more avenues around this issue, and learn more about different kinds of work that is being done to eradicate it. I plan to engage in even more conversation, attend more talks and discussions around sexual assault and violence. I want to learn how to better lift up victims and survivors alike, how to advocate for them, and how to be what they need in a friend, not just for the friends I already have, but for everyone I might cross paths with in the future.

I think that it is important in making a plan for myself going forward, I adequately evaluate the path ahead, and myself in doing so. To do this I will use something we use often within Justice and Peace Studies, a S.W.O.T. Analysis. S.W.O.T. stands for Strengths, Weaknesses, Opportunities, and Threats.

I think that the strengths I have going forward are the different connections I have made since my time at St. Thomas as a Justice and Peace Studies major. Like I mentioned above, I have found friends, classmates, peers, professors, and met people like Sarah, who share interests, passions, and goals that are very similar to mine. They are a great resource for me, in all I can learn from them, and the advice I can get going forward. In my experience, the people you keep around you are the ones who really make the journey, and I feel really good about the company I keep.

Of course, in any endeavor there are weaknesses, in my case they are personal. With frequency, I find myself struggling to know what the right thing to say is. Whether that be in calling someone out for their behavior, or a comment they made, or just engaging in a conversation with someone who doesn't see eye to eye with me. This is not because I don't want to speak up, or challenge and be challenged, but because I know I am likely to be met with resistance, and when conversations get difficult, I sometimes struggle to find the words I want. I am not an expert, and often doubt myself, my knowledge and my ability to hold up to people. I question my validity. This is a weakness that is a work in progress, but work that I welcome.

The opportunity portion of a S.W.O.T. analysis is my absolute favorite part. Unlike strengths, weaknesses, it is imaginative, and futuristic. Opportunities for me are what's to come, the possibilities the future might hold, and the exploration of the unknown. In my case the opportunities I have that are placed right in front of me on campus at UST to engage in discussions, dialogues, to attend talks or lectures, and learn skills are ever present. Over time I have begun taking more advantage of these events that engage and interest me, however I think that the best is actually beyond this campus. I have found opportunity here at school without even looking, so what opportunity and resources I will find with some more digging is what really excites me.

The unfortunate reality I face in the journey ahead, is that there will be things that threaten my progress. However, I think the biggest threat to me is the status quo. Change and growth do not occur by staying put or staying comfortable, and though sometimes this is the easiest option, it can be a dangerous pattern to fall into. One of safety, and security. I have seen myself succumb to this many times before, and I am sure I will again, however breaking this habit, and consistently checking in on myself is important in combating this. I have challenged myself to get out of my comfort zone, put myself out there, and grow. There will be slip-ups, and I will need to take breaks, but I am optimistic about what lies ahead, and my ability to face it in whatever form it takes.

A S.W.O.T. analysis is a valuable tool that is used in assessing companies, organizations, non-profits, and even conflicts, but in my case, I think it is most impactful in evaluating myself. I challenge others who find themselves impassioned about an area of injustice to not only embark on a journey toward growth and advocacy, but not to forget to engage in self-reflection and evaluation along the way.

Works Cited

Lederach, J. P. (2005). *The moral imagination.* New York, NY: Oxford University Press.

About the Author – Sidney Severson

I am a Junior at the University of St. Thomas, majoring in Justice and Peace Studies with a concentration in Conflict Analysis and Transformation, and a minor in Sociology.

Tree Trust: Improving Lives and Landscapes
Paige Hietpas

Circle round for freedom, circle round for peace.
For all of us imprisoned, circle for release.
Circle for the planet, circle for each soul.
For the children of our children, keep the circle whole.
—Singing the Living Tradition

Story

Despite maximum effort by cities to prevent Dutch elm disease from taking over in the 1970's, the spread of its fungus allowed the disease to slowly devastate the Twin Cities metro area's elm canopy. As the environmental devastation increased, so did youth unemployment rates, as the American economy was not in good shape. It seemed very unlikely that these challenges would ever lead to something good. Don Willeke, a liberal democrat, and Rolf Svedsen, an active republican, saw these needs and reacted to them. They founded Tree Trust in 1976 and, despite different backgrounds, grounded themselves in their common goals and their mission to improve the landscape by investing in people.

It started big. In just the first year, Tree Trust employed 1,450 youth in Suburban Hennepin county. There were no obstacles to regulatory job training forms such as the I-9 and public funding was readily available. To respond to Dutch Elm disease, youth crews were tasked with taking care of new seedlings in municipal tree nurseries;

nurturing and maintaining them by watering and weeding, securing their roots with burlap, then planting them in surrounding communities and city parks.

While this work was incredibly valuable, Tree Trust quickly realized that having young people upkeep nurseries for nine weeks was not really doing much for them in terms of job training and development. St. Louis Parks' Westwood Hills Nature Center changed that. In 1978, a youth crew dedicated their time to constructing a boardwalk across a lake there. One by one, they built every section by hand. They used no power equipment, just manual tools and human drive. The participants familiarized themselves with carpenter saws, bits and braces, hammers, etc. And, they learned to really work as a team. After building each section, they would swim it out and attach it onto the section before. Soon, they had completely constructed a 1,480-foot boardwalk.

Outsiders were awed by the results. Other parks reached out saying "I didn't think you had the resources to do that" or "Who did this for you?" Tree Trust was suddenly in demand because of their committed labor force and their willingness to try new projects. The organization evolved to employ students who were underserved and hadn't seen a lot of success in their lives, facing barriers to employment such as low income, special needs, or having been in the juvenile justice system.

Their organization has grown, metaphorically, into a tree, in which leadership stems into different branches: Employment Programs, Development and Communications, Finance & Human Resources, Community Forestry, Operations and Landscape Services and Project Development & IT. Stemming from employment programs, there are four program leaders who narrow their attention in on the five programs which Tree Trust offers: Community Support Program, Youth Conservation Corps, Youth & Young Adult Services, YouthBuild, and Landscape Services. Within these individual programs, there are leaders which make them run smoothly, including crew leaders, counselors, project site supervisors, tutors, etc. However, the real work comes from those that are employed in the programs. They carry the work out in a way that makes them leaders with power to make the organization what it is.

Summer 2017 - Paige's work at MN Valley National Wildlife Refuge

Norm Champ, the current executive director at Tree Trust, points out that "the ones that stick with it, with staff support, get so much out of it because they didn't think they could do it… but then they did it." He points to the importance of them taking advantage of the opportunities that lie ahead of them. Tree Trust gets them on their feet, teaching them valuable employment skills for the future. To guide them in this process, motivational interviewing is used to allow space for the youth to make their own steps toward progress. This approach encourages making positive decisions and accomplishing established goals and steers them away from indecision and uncertainty. Ultimately, it helps them recognize their assets and realize their potential for success.

Central to the organization's mission is the Youth Conservation Corps, which has been around since the beginning. On a basic level, each of the crew members bring their own assets of a wide variety to this work, from the ability to use tools and calculate measurements on projects, to teamwork and relating to co-workers. In the first weeks of work, youth discover what they like and what they are good at and they bring those skills to the workplace. On an organizational level, the asset that Tree Trust brings is their ability to demonstrate to workers that they each have assets that are useful and valuable. Sometimes the assets appear to be negative, but even they can be turned around. At the very least, they are taught to give it their best.

I have personally seen this work come to life. Last summer, I worked as a crew leader for Tree Trust at the Minnesota Valley Wildlife Refuge in Bloomington. Each morning, I would pick my crew up from their school and bring them to their natural work place for a full day. Most of them had never experienced the outdoors quite like this. Over the course of the summer, we put in a 100-foot timber hand rail along an overlook and completely re-built a large fishing platform. In addition, they learned how to put in erosion control alongside the pond and got to plant wild grasses and flowers to beautify the area. I witnessed my teams grow tremendously in their communication skills, relationship building, tool use and their connection to the natural world. Just to watch a crew member hammer in a stake for the first time or use a pick ax to deconstruct (safely) a rotted out bench was very moving. Some days, they worked and improved on resume building, budgeting and career exploration. When the end of summer came, I was sad to say goodbye, but happy knowing that they were on a better track and had successfully put in their own parts to the project, feeling accomplished and excited.

Summer 2017 - Paige's work at MN Valley National Wildlife Refuge

From my experience, it was clear to me that Tree Trust meets their crew members where they are at while challenging them to grow in other areas. Champ tells the story of a kid with one arm that might have struggled to complete other tasks, but he took on sweeping steps during the work project. It was a long staircase. He accepted the challenge and embodied it as his own job. This is one of thousands of examples over the 41 years where kids thrive in the work environment because they learn how to use their own skills and find a desire to learn. They are also taught to get along with coworkers and listen to and respect the employer. They are being paid to be there, so if they don't do so, there are consequences, including being fired. They learn to recognize and hone their assets. By guiding this process, Tree Trust engages with the conflict of youth unemployment by helping them learn valuable job skills. At the same time, they are improving the landscape.

Theory

There has been a re-evaluation when it comes to community development. In the past, typically, outside help was sent to deal with identified problems. This most often did not work as it focused mainly on what was missing or problematic. A newer way of thinking is assets-based community development. In this approach, the assets present in the community - the capacities of the people and the associational and institutional base of the area - are identified. These assets are strengthened by improving capacities and by building relationships between resources (Kretzmann & McKnight 1996, 23) which increases their effectiveness by multiples. In this model, all people bring value of their own and are included, even those that have been marginalized in the past. The handicapped or disabled, those experiencing low-income, the old and young, are all brought into the effort (Kretzmann & McKnight 1996, p. 26). Getting a commitment from local people to invest in themselves and their resources provides the opportunity to rebuild lives and the community. The people become contributors to the community building process and to society rather than being stagnated as recipients of outside help. Outside help has a place in this asset-based model, but as an assistance rather than a solution. As the community begins to rebuild, strengths and assets can be matched in new ways, relationships are built and rebuilt, and there are new sources of income and a host of new possibilities for the future. It is a continuing process, evident in the structure and history of Tree Trust.

In many ways, Tree Trust employs this assets-based approach in carrying out their work. From the experiences I have had with Tree Trust, I have a better understanding of how their model has grown to be successful. Tree Trust believes that all youth and young adults have assets, but have never had the channels in which to direct them. The programs that Tree Trust offers highlight youth abilities and strengths and puts them to use. Despite real differences of abilities and personal background, participants bring energy and a variety of skills and they learn to work together to ultimately better the wider community environment. Together, the youth and young adults work to better their community's landscape while at the same time experiencing self-growth and an improvement in their employment capabilities.

There are many examples in which we can see the assets-based approach taking place. At Tree Trust, they really push the employees to utilize gifts that are within themselves to complete the work and build their community. For example, there may be a kid who has a physical disability, but who can still help out on the project in smaller, but equally meaningful, ways. They are never denied because of a barrier they may face. Tree Trust helps them overcome their hurdles by showing them that they can do the work, and do it well, if they really try. This results in successful and long-lasting landscaping projects which are built by hands which were believed to be incapable before their involvement with Tree Trust. They are no longer treated as marginalized people, but rather as employees who have the means and resources they need to be successful.

Another example is the deep and active listening that takes place with those who enter into the program. Listening is a key principle to the assets-based approach because it is person-centered and allows the employees to really be heard. Tree Trust engages its staff in motivational interviewing with those who need the inspiration to find the change within themselves. While other interventions are about giving information and taking interviewees through particular strategies, motivational interviewing shows that the person doing the interviewing is not the expert. Rather, they are seen as peers and equals.

Clients thus look inward at their own resources and skills that they can call upon to do the job. These tactics fully engage the person in their journey to use their own recognized assets to better their lives and their communities.

Tree Trust does utilize additional resources from the outside in the form of federal aid and donations. But, since the community is invested and mobilized, these resources are used more effectively than had they just been used in traditional ways. On their own, these funds would not be sufficient enough to meet the challenges of the community let alone elicit the change that is brought about with the Tree Trust programs (Kretzmann & McKnight 1996, p. 23).

These improved lives and landscapes follow the youth and young adults into their futures and go hand-in-hand with leadership for social justice. Youth are given a voice on their projects and their futures; they are not left silenced. This leads to more active participation in society through the workforce. They figure out what is right for them, what skills they have, how to work under an employer, and how to maintain relationships with others in the community. These realizations help them integrate into the community for the betterment of all. The successful results that Tree Trust has had over their forty-plus years is a testament to how well the assets-based community development approach can work.

Action Planning

Looking forward another forty-plus years, the SWOT analysis can be a helpful framework for Tree Trust to consider their strengths, weaknesses and opportunities, as well as the threats they face. By conducting a SWOT analysis, Tree Trust can look at what about their organization is working for or against them. This tool can be used to build understanding of the potential Tree Trust has for growth.

Tree Trust has a lot of strength in their well-trained support staff and leadership. Each group and individual within the organization compliments the others and, in collective effort, they are able to provide meaningful opportunities for those who seek services from them. There is a lot of trust built among staff to do the work well and to ask for assistance when it is needed. Champ himself, as the executive director, understands that people have their own areas of expertise and lets those who are under his leadership really take charge of their work. As mentioned earlier, because they have such a solid support staff, the different areas of the organization operate well together. The employees even help in areas of the organization outside of their own. Whether it is a weekend spent planting trees or stuffing envelopes with checks for crew members, they take care to work together.

Because of these different areas working together, Tree Trust shows strength in their ability to fully engage with both the natural environment and the social. They have become valued in Minnesota for all of their success stories and their long-standing relationships. Tree Trust continuously puts out quality work and has a very good reputation with local communities and parks. These are continued connections that they have built and maintained over the past forty-one years which have resulted in the improvement of a lot of lives and landscapes. Champ quotes one of his counselors saying: "If you want to know the extent of Tree Trust, wear a Tree Trust shirt to the Minnesota State Fair. You can't go ten feet without someone stopping you to tell you their connection to the organization." This shows that longevity has created a bigger impact.

While there are a lot of strengths that the organization embodies, this does not mean that there are not weaknesses. One weakness is that the demographics of crew leaders and counselors are often not equitably representative of the youth and young adults that Tree Trust works with. This might be because of the ways Tree Trust recruits their summer staff and short-term employees from universities. Representation could affect the way that participants in the programs feel connected to their leaders, counselors, and tutors. If someone does not have a similar background as you, it is harder to relate and it could be harder to trust in them.

Another weakness is that often the programming with youth is not as focused on trees as it used to be. More specifically, the Youth

Conservation Corps has for the most part moved to be about conservation construction projects, like building retaining walls, handrails, and paver paths in parks, rather than just planting trees. In a lot of ways this is a good thing, as the youth gain a lot more employment skills in these environments than they would in a tree nursery, but with the Emerald Ash Borer (EAB) looming and becoming more and more common in Minnesota, this could be seen as a weakness: to not have more hands-on deck clearing and replanting. Most of that work is done by the forestry division and volunteers. However, this could be an opportunity for Tree Trust, to move back to that old model for a little while to confront the EAB issue that is presenting itself and rising rapidly. There will always be a youth employment need. But, with the rise in EAB, Tree Trust's forestry division is going to have to respond in full-force and they could use the help of the people in the job training division to do so. Somehow the organization needs to find a balance between the response to this disaster and job training for youth and young adults.

This opportunity to switch gears brings to light threats and barriers that Tree Trust has faced and is facing. At the core of the threats is funding. Tree Trust operates on mostly government grants for low income and special needs job programming, and also on contributions from individual donors. Most of this money goes directly to the summer programs as it is the biggest part of Tree Trust. However, the money gets sucked up fast and they cannot employ nearly as many kids as they used to, especially since they are working at a rising minimum wage. As stated earlier, the first year Tree Trust operated, they were able to employ 1,450 kids in Hennepin county. Now, they can only employ about 100 at minimum wage. Even as minimum wage is rising, the funding has gone down, although the need is still there for employment skills programming.

States have not given enough funding to cities to fully address the EAB issue. Tree Trust is perfectly positioned to take care of the disaster that is already there, it just needs more money to do so, especially if it's going to be connected again with the employment skills programming. These are hard threats to face, as they determine the direction Tree Trust will go now. However, applying this SWOT analysis to Tree Trust offers a guide for creating a strategy going forward.

Tree Trust can rely on their broad mission statement while exploring new opportunities going forward. They should look outside of themselves to start working with more advocacy organizations for funding in either the social or the environmental arena. Or, they could begin from the inside by exploring their different options for fundraising amongst their forty-plus years of connections. Whatever their strategy becomes, it will need to focus on enhancing its strengths, learning from its weaknesses, taking its opportunities, while managing and eliminating threats. By doing so, Tree Trust will be able to continue its success into the future.

Works Cited

Kretzmann, J. & McKnight, J.P. (1996). Assets-based community development. *National Civic Review* 85.4: 23-28.
N. Champ, personal communication, October 9, 2017.

About the Author – Paige Hietpas

Saint Paul born and raised, I am now on my 21st year in the area. To stick close to my beautifully large family, I chose to go to the University of St. Thomas where I am in my 4th and final year double majoring in Justice & Peace Studies and Environmental Studies and minoring in Spanish. I am very involved on campus programs, but outside of my school life you can usually find me hikin', rock collectin', scrapbookin' and eatin' peanut butter and pickle sandwiches (Grammie's favorite).

When I was little, my grandparents started a nonprofit called the Nandale Foundation which aims to foster respect for the environment and promote initiatives to improve and protect the natural world. Starting at quite a young age, I was on the junior board of the foundation and was writing grant proposals for the places that I was passionate about. Through my involvement in that foundation, my membership in a Unitarian Universalist congregation and my upbringing in a Spanish immersion school, I spent my childhood inspired by many amazing people. From these individuals, I have learned that anyone can be a leader. To me, leadership is about sharing your light and passions with the world, and allowing the light of others to shine in. This fosters a sense of belonging, community, and reciprocal responsibility in the work for common goals.

Vietnamese Social Services of Minnesota
Joanna Larson

Story

In 1975, the capital of South Vietnam fell to the North Vietnam troops, drawing the Vietnam War to a close. With the end of the War came a wave of Vietnamese refugees fleeing the Northern rule. Some of these refugees settled down in Minnesota and a small population began to grow.

Relocating to America was not easy. Many came because of fear for their wellbeing and life, not because they wanted to. Refugees lost their place in society and missed their homeland.
Coming from Vietnam to the United States there were a lot of new things to learn. A new language, new systems, new skills and more were various challenges that refugees had to face and adapt to.

To address the issue of adjustment, a group of community leaders came together and established the Vietnamese Social Services of Minnesota (VSS) in 1987. The organization started out small, offering only one service, an elder program. It focused on the older generation of refugees, who had lost their high level of social status when coming to the United States. The program worked to socialize the elders and helped them access social assistance benefits. Since then, VSS has grown to offer multiple programs that span a wide spectrum of social services. Currently, VSS offers programs such as job training, youth programs, health services, English learning and more.

I interviewed one of VSS's dedicated employees, Dung Phan, who oversees the health services of VSS. She helped build the program from the ground up, working at VSS since 1998. When she arrived at VSS she started out with working with the Elder program, but after six months she shifted to work on health. At the time, VSS did not offer any health programs or services. Dung had a degree in computer science and was not experienced in health, but it was a program that she felt passionate about. Dung was a refugee herself; her father had been a political prisoner held in the "re-education" camps in Vietnam, which were inhumane prisons run by the Vietnamese Communist government after the war. Dung was driven to learn about health services because she had a strong desire to help her people. She took health classes at a local college and educated herself on the Minnesota health system. With her education, Dung was able to create the VSS health services.

Dung has helped her people. Through her job she has helped thousands of immigrants and refugees gain health insurance and services. She assists in scheduling doctor's appointments, provides chemically dependency resources, coordinates flu clinics, and so much more. In 2016 alone, she assisted 2,600 refugees and immigrants in getting health insurance through MNsure, Minnesota's health coverage marketplace.

In addition to overseeing health services, Dung is a reference for people to go to. She often talks to immigrants and refugees and answers their questions about America: basic questions such as, *How does 911 work?* Or *What is terrorism?* She also deals with more complex question too, like how to vote. During our short interview, there were several clients that popped in just to say hi and chat. Dung has made a positive impact in many people's lives.

VSS started out by only providing services only to Vietnamese people but over the years, VSS has grown to accommodate more refugee groups. The Karen people are an ethnic group from Myanmar who fled due to civil war and persecution. Many lived in refugee camps in Thailand, but some have relocated to Minnesota and other parts of the US. In the United States, Minnesota has the largest Karen population with numbers around 14,000 in St. Paul. Minnesota also has a large Somali population that VSS serves. Like the Karen, many refugees come from Somalia to flee civil war and violence.

The English as a Second Language (ESL) classes are one of the programs that brings all the nationalities together, learning side by side. Language is vital skill that many new immigrants and refugees need to learn so that they can find employment and navigate society. ESL classes at VSS provide this service, offering multiple classes that cater to different proficiency levels.

The English learning program provides a comfortable environment for people to learn. The classroom is often filled with laughter and comradery. Pieces of American culture are woven into lessons to provide immigrants and refugees more understanding of the country they are living in. Teachers point out information that might be obvious to American citizens, but is unknown to some immigrants, like multiple time zones in the same country, not sitting down at a table that has a "reserved" sign on it, and what frostbite is.

Through their programs, VSS helps refugees and immigrants adjust to life in the United States. It can be a difficult transition to leave home and VSS works to help ease that change. VSS has helped thousands of people over the years and will continue to help thousands more.

Theory

John Paul Lederach's Web of Relationships illustrates how VSS works to create social change. In his book, *The Moral Imagination* (2005), Lederach describes the Web of Relationships as making a web, or social network, to create social change, building relationships and connections like a spider creates a web. VSS creates and builds off relationships and uses those relationships to accomplish more than they could on their own. It is through these relationships that social change can be created and grow (pp.75-86). The more connections and strands the web has the stronger the web, and the more effective it is. The more connections and allies VSS has the more they can offer to immigrants and refugees. During our interview, Dung highlighted the importance of the connections she builds and how they improve her ability to do her job. VSS builds a variety of relationships to help meet different needs that immigrants and refugees have and provide resources for them.

One type of relationship VSS builds is with other organizations. They work with multiple programs to expand their resource base and offer more services to immigrants and refugees. VSS partners with the Minnesota Literacy Council to help find and train volunteers to help out with the English Language Learning classes. VSS also works with international groups to identify incoming refugees so they can meet them at the airport and be with the refugees to help them navigate an unfamiliar country. Additionally, VSS connects with temples in the community as a lot of their outreach is done through temples. In a spider's web, these organizations would be the anchor threads that are attached to fixed points. These strands touch all different areas and provide support and stability to VSS as well as providing more opportunities to make connections.

VSS's Self-Sufficiency program works to get immigrants and refugees to support themselves through job training and job placement. To help accomplish this, development staff at VSS have established many relationships with companies around the Twin Cities area to place their clients into jobs. These relationships are important as they are companies that are willing to hire immigrants and refugees that may lack high levels of skill and experience.

Another relationship that is important to VSS is the relationship to the state of Minnesota and its institutions. VSS works with schools to assist kids in overcoming language barriers and adjust to the United States. They also work with different counties to help overcome the language barrier with probation officers and in other areas as needed. At one of the VSS events, they brought in mayoral candidates running in the upcoming election to talk to the elder circle. One more important connection is the public housing system which VSS works with to help immigrants and refugees find affordable housing. These relationships strengthen VSS's network and helps the web function.

Finally, one of the most important relationships that VSS creates is with the immigrants and refugees they serve. In the course of a year VSS provides resources for 4,000-5,000 people. Not only does VSS help people in the Twin Cities area, but they connect with immigrants and refugees all over the state. VSS builds relationships between its staff and its clients. One way they connect is through events. In the English Language Learning classes, the teachers at VSS put on a Thanksgiving lunch and invited all their students. The teachers brought food and served their students. Through these relationships, VSS builds a community that stays connected throughout the years. As some refugees and immigrants move away strands of the web do sometimes weaken. However, new strands are constantly being created as new people locate in Minnesota and find assistance in VSS.

VSS started off as a small organization, but as time went on and the need grew, VSS grew as well, building connections which gave VSS the ability to serve more and more people. Over the years VSS has expanded their connections and continue to create more services. They started by focusing on one need, supporting elders, and from that they have continued to expand outward. Continuing with Lederach's web analogy, it is like how a spider creates its web, starting off with a simple base and continuing to add more threads and more connections to build a sturdier and more effective web. Building relationships is an important and vital part of Dung's and other VSS employees work. Organizations that connect with VSS are building their Web of Relationships as well. They do not have to do everything on their own but can rely on others to provide help. The Web of Relationships has many benefits that help create social change.

Action Plan

When looking at how an organization can build off of what they have accomplished, the SWOT analysis is helpful. SWOT looks at the strengths, weaknesses, opportunities, and threats of an organization. From this analysis, areas that need to be built on can be identified and action plans can be created. It is useful method to examine VSS and see where they are doing well and where they could use some improvement and move forward from there.

VSS has a lot of strengths that they use to their advantage. The organization currently does a lot of great things for immigrants and refugees. They have a network of partnerships with organizations and people that they use provide many different services that cover a broad range of needs and age groups. Throughout their existence, VSS has consistently and effectively expanded their network to include more clients and more allies. Another strength is VSS's dedicated staff who work hard and care deeply about their clients. Their staff is knowledgeable and have a lot experience in what they do.

One weakness that faces VSS is their ability to reach immigrants and refugees around the state. VSS concentrates its resources in the Twin Cities because of their location in St. Paul and because populations of immigrants and refugees are concentrated in the Twin Cities. However, there are populations spread across Minnesota. VSS does have contact with them through phone calls, but it can be harder to reach them beyond that. In the past, VSS did provide person to person services for immigrants and refugees in St. Cloud, but could not sustain those services due to funding.

VSS has opportunities to grow by continuing to add people to their programs. Assisting groups that are outside of their original Vietnamese population, such as the Karen people, has contributed to reaching more people. This can be seen in the frequency of new students joining the English learning classes. The organization might consider taking on even more groups. Everyone that VSS assists and works with is an opportunity for VSS to expand their network.

There are a couple of threats that VSS faces, a broad threat and one that is more immediate. The immediate threat VSS has to deal with is funding, which is an issue that a lot of organizations have to face. During our interview, Dung mentioned that some of their funding from the government had been cut, which limited the organization's work. VSS relies heavily on government funding, so they could consider diversifying their funds. VSS might look towards donors, whether individuals or organizations, or hold fundraising events like a call-a-thon or a donation dinner. Creating new funding strength is a difficult problem and can be very challenging to overcome.

A broad threat to VSS is the negativity that some people feel about refugees and immigrants. This negativity seems to increasingly have a louder and louder voice. The current U.S. administration has created policies designed to keep people out and has promoted a rhetoric of exclusion and xenophobia. There is potential that the United States will become a hostile place for immigrants and refugees. Some outcomes of this negatively might be that it becomes harder for immigrants and refugees to come to the United States and become citizens, or government funding that benefits refugees and immigrants might continue to be cut. These are only a couple of the possible outcomes and there are likely many more negative consequences due to anti-outsider feelings.

While this threat is far reaching and one that VSS cannot solve on its own, VSS can contribute to improving the situation. VSS might accomplish this is by approaching the issue through grassroots work, aiming at changing and improving attitudes in people in the surrounding community. Affecting the attitudes of community members will hopefully lead to affecting their government leaders and influencing government policy. Additionally, community members have the power to reflect their views and ideas to their family and friends which would hopefully widen the positive influence of grassroots work.

A way that VSS might approach building relationships with the surrounding community is by creating interaction between the two groups. VSS could host cultural events and invite the surrounding community. This would be a way to create positive experiences as well as a way to share culture. Another event VSS could possibly do would be a story event, where immigrants and refugees share their stories. This might help promote more awareness of hardships that immigrants and refugees go through and gain sympathy. If done well, live storytelling has the potential to be massively impactful. To make things easier for themselves, VSS could host the events alongside organizations they that are already partners, and organizations who engage in storytelling work. These are only a few ideas and there are many other options that VSS could pursue to promote community interaction.

Examining the strengths, weaknesses, opportunities, and threats of VSS, new opportunities and directions can be identified. The solutions proposed are my suggestions and VSS staff or supporters using the SWOT analysis might have different ideas on how to move forward. Either way, SWOT analysis is a useful tool that can help an organization recognize what they are doing well and generate ways they can continue to improve.

Works Cited

Lederach, J. P. (2005). The moral imagination: the art and the soul of building peace. Oxford: University Press.

About the Author – Joanna Larson

I am a junior at the University of St. Thomas and I plan on graduating in 2019. I am majoring in International Studies with a focus on Political Science.

We Are All Criminals
Mary Halonen

One in four people in the U.S. has a criminal record.
Four in four have a criminal history.

Story

People with criminal records have many barriers in front of them, whether it be prejudice or discrimination against them on an individual level, or on an institutional level. On an individual level, this can manifest itself in ways such as others refusing to interact with a person or having a negative perception of them, but on an institutional level, it can prevent people from renting a house or apartment, finding a job, or even from voting. This leaves people with a criminal record unable to support themselves or their families by any legal means, creating an incentive for recidivism (re-offense of a crime), creating a cycle of crime that is very difficult to break. The NAACP has found that "a criminal record can reduce the likelihood of a callback or job offer by nearly 50 percent" (Criminal Justice Fact Sheet, 2017). This statistic shows just how large of a problem this is, and how hard it is for people with criminal records to re-enter society. These issues and barriers are a central part of why We Are All Criminals was founded.

We Are All Criminals is a project that was developed to "[challenge] society's perception of what it means to be a criminal" (About, 2017). The project was founded by Emily Baxter, who had previously been a public defender before starting a job at a non-profit, working to help people with criminal records get expungements. It was in this position that Emily really recognized the privilege she had in not having a criminal record; she was able to forget any mistakes or criminal actions she had made because she was never caught but the people she served were not easily able to do the same. From this began

We Are All Criminals: "For the past few years, I've been asking people like me—the 75% of people in the US with criminal histories but no record: What have you had the luxury to forget?" (Baxter, 2017).

    I spoke with Richard McLemore III, the Vice Chair of We Are All Criminals – WAAC, for short – about the project and his involvement with it. Richard began working with WAAC because he felt the organization he worked for beforehand did not have a passion for re-entry work, but WAAC did. Richard has a criminal background, so he is affected by the issues that WAAC faces. If he were to somehow lose his job or housing, he could face barriers in finding an employer or landlord who would work around his criminal record, even though the record is over twenty years old. Richard explained that his criminal background initially did not help his perspective about the issues of re-entry and perceptions, but he realized that he "had a lot to learn about the criminal justice system outside of [his] small point of view" (McLemore, 2017). WAAC works to educate people about these issues and to open up a conversation about privilege, power, and how people really feel about the issues. Richard explained that part of WAAC's social justice goal is to "[give] people a space to address how they really feel," (McLemore, 2017) so that people can recognize that their own ways of thinking might not address the whole story and hear differing opinions and ways of thinking. Another important point Richard mentioned was that WAAC wants to "keep open lines of communication for everybody, not just folks who already believe in what we're doing, because we understand in order to change minds we have to be inclusive" (McLemore, 2017). Inclusivity is crucial when looking to alter the way society thinks and acts, because it allows for all different sides to come together and work past their differences. In order to achieve their goals, WAAC uses various platforms, from community engagement, to a newly published book, to social media; and all decisions are made by the board by majority vote.

    This project has been largely successful in changing the mindsets and perspectives of people about what it means to have a criminal record. One of the most common reactions that people have to WAAC is a realization of their own privilege, as many of the people who engage with WAAC's projects are people who do not have a criminal record. Like most people, many participants have committed actions in their lifetime that would be considered criminal, but were never caught or punished. According to Richard, people explain that they hadn't thought about their criminal actions for many years and that "it was no big deal," but WAAC helps them realize there are people suffering for the same or similar actions, simply because they had been caught. The realization that a person could be in the same situation as someone with a criminal record if they had simply gotten punished for their actions works to change the perspective that people with criminal records are "bad guys". Though there is still much work to be done, so that people with criminal records no longer face barriers to re-entering society, changing society's perspective about what it means to have, or not to have, a criminal record is a step in the right direction.

Theory

The danger of a single story is a simple concept, but it's importance is often overlooked. Author Chimamanda Ngozi Adichie explains that a single story only provides one perspective or idea about a problem, a person, or a situation, even though there is almost always more than one side to a story. For Adichie, the danger was that all of the stories she knew were about British or American people or topics. Until she discovered other Nigerian writers, she was unaware that stories could be about people like her (Adichie, 2009). The danger of a single story for We Are All Criminals is that if society recognizes people with criminal records only as criminals they are ignoring that there is more to a person, and that it does not define who someone is.

We Are All Criminals' goal in providing an alternative to the single story is to "[challenge] society's perception of what it means to be a criminal" (About, 2017). To do this, they use storytelling among other forms of teaching to educate society and to tell various sides of a previously one-sided story. The single story that many people believe is that people with criminal records are "bad guys" who are committing crime simply because they do not have morals or because they are evil. This story comes from the media, from movies and TV shows, even from authority figures. When people believe this one-sided story, they are missing the part of the narrative that illustrates who a person is outside of their criminal record, or the circumstances that may have drawn them to commit a crime out of necessity. By encouraging people to reframe the single story they have likely been told throughout their lives, WAAC allows a fuller story to be told, one that humanizes people who have criminal records while also showing those who do not have criminal records that they may be just as guilty of a crime as those who do.

The danger of a single story for people with criminal records is that it often prevents them from being employed, finding housing, or voting, among many other barriers (Berson, 2013). Decision makers, along with average people, often believe stereotypes and stigmas about people with criminal histories, and this belief leads them to continue practices that bar people with criminal records from successfully re-entering society. As Richard McLemore explained during our interview, many people had not thought about the fact that they had committed criminal actions, or what the implications of those actions could have been had they been caught (McLemore, 2017). WAAC opens another side of the story that allows people to recognize that people with criminal records are no different than themselves.

From Adichie's explanation of the dangers of a single story and WAAC's efforts to reframe individuals' perspectives regarding criminals, it is apparent how damaging it is to only learn a single story. We should strive to see more than one side of a story in all circumstances to better understand the complexity of others and how our knowledge of something often does not represent the entire story. This concept is especially important in a leadership setting, as leaders often have the opportunity and responsibility to make decisions based on their experience and on the stories that they know and have been told. Acknowledging another story besides their own can happen in the form of listening to others with different viewpoints, experiencing firsthand situations other than theirs, or by taking the time to educate themselves on a topic they may not know about. By doing any of these actions before making decisions, a leader no longer falls subject to the danger of a single story, as they understand multiple viewpoints and can therefore make more informed decisions that could affect a group, an organization, a country, or the world.

Collective Action

The Circle of Praxis exemplifies the way We Are All Criminals has worked to reach their goals and to be a leader for social justice. The steps of the Circle of Praxis are insertion, descriptive analysis, normative analysis, and action possibilities. Insertion involves inserting oneself into a situation of injustice, followed by descriptive analysis, which is an analysis of the societal structures that lead to this injustice. Next, the normative analysis works to challenge the norms of society that perpetuate injustice. Finally, in the action possibilities step, work is done to identify potential action that can be made to end the injustice that is being faced. These steps help to guide the work done by WAAC. The first step of the Circle of Praxis, "insertion," can be seen in WAAC's work as the personal experiences of those working for the organization, such as Richard McLemore's firsthand experience with the criminal justice system or Emily Baxter's experience working to help people who have had firsthand experience with the system. Insertion is also exemplified in participants' experiences of WAAC that educate them about injustices faced by people with criminal records. This insertion into injustice is what led to the creation of WAAC and has inspired a "descriptive analysis" into the power structures and societal ideas that lead to negative perceptions and treatment of people who have criminal records. The "normative analysis" aspect of the Circle of Praxis relates to the work that WAAC has done to find the most effective ways to work with communities to change individual perspectives from what is accepted as being normal, or the stereotypical idea that people hold, to seeing both sides of the story. Which then leads to the "action planning" step to put these realizations into action. WAAC has taken many steps to create positive social change, and there is still much to be done.

Many of the steps that WAAC has taken can be found within the Social Change Wheel (Klein, 2017). The parts of the wheel that seem to most accurately fit with the actions of WAAC are education and community building, which seem to work hand in hand within WAAC's approach, through their actions that have been discussed previously, such as exhibits, speaking events, and conversations with the public that are meant to provide people with new ideas and perceptions other than those perpetuated by negative stereotypes. These aspects are also seen through WAAC's efforts to involve employers, landlords, educators, and students in this movement. On their website, www.weareallcriminals.org/get-involved, the organization's "Get Involved" page includes steps that each of these groups can take to lessen the barriers that people with criminal records face in re-entry. For employers, fair hiring policies are provided on the webpage, along with suggestions such as removing criminal history requirements from job applications or tailoring background checks to fit the employers' specific needs, along with educational resources for employers who would like to learn more. Landlords are provided with steps that they can take to fairly assess applicants who have criminal records, instead of turning an applicant away without understanding the nature of their conviction or whether it is relevant to their tenancy. Finally, WAAC provides resources for students and educators to get involved and to learn more about the issue and about programs that work towards creating justice for people facing barriers in re-entry.

An aspect of the Social Change Wheel that could aid in WAAC's mission is grassroots political organizing. Grassroots organizing involves coming together as a community to make a change, fitting into WAAC's work to invite the community into a space of open learning and understanding. A grassroots approach for WAAC could involve campaigning or lobbying for legislators to change current laws regarding the barriers that those who have criminal records face, such as voting laws or background checks for employment or renting a home or apartment. For example, current laws allow landlords to use criminal background checks to screen out applicants, preventing many people with criminal records from being able to find housing. Additionally, when looking for employment, many who have a criminal record are screened out by potential employers after background checks inform the employers of a criminal record. These barriers make it incredibly hard for many who have criminal records to reenter society; uniting people who have criminal records and their allies through grassroots organizing would give WAAC the opportunity to work towards making a change in the way that these laws negatively affect people with criminal records. Further, by changing these laws it would help to eliminate the negative stereotypes that many individuals in society hold. By combining the strategies that We Are All Criminals already uses, and adding an additional strategy from the Social Change Wheel, they will be able to create a greater impact in pursuit of their mission.

Works Cited

About. (2017) We Are All Criminals, Retrieved from www.weareallcriminals.org/about/.

Adichie, Chimamanda N. (2009). Chimamanda Ngozi Adichie: The danger of a single story [Video file]. Retrieved from https://www.ted.com/talks/chimamanda_adichie_the_danger_of_a_single_story/

Baxter, Emily. How WAAC Began. We Are All Criminals, Retrieved from www.weareallcriminals.com/how-waac-began/.

Berson, Sarah B. (2013). Beyond the Sentence - Understanding Collateral Consequences. National Institute of Justice, 272.

Criminal Justice Fact Sheet. NAACP (2017). Retrieved from www.naacp.org/criminal-justice-fact-sheet/.

Get Involved. (2017) We Are All Criminals, Retrieved from www.weareallcriminals.org/getinvolved/.

Klein, M. (2017). Social change wheel analysis: Beyond the dichotomy of charity or justice, in Colon, C.; Gristwood, A. & Woolf, M. (2017). Civil Rights and Inequalities, Occasional Publication #6, Boston: CAPA, The Global Education Network.

McLemore, R. (2017, October 18). Personal Interview.

About the Author – Mary Halonen

I am senior at the University of St. Thomas studying Criminal Justice. I've been passionate about justice issues for as long as I can remember, and I hope to spend my life focused on finding solutions to injustice in the world. On campus, you can usually find me in class or at meetings for Students for Justice and Peace, and off campus, you can find me outside (when it's not freezing – thanks Minnesota winters), or at a coffee shop, trying to find the best espresso possible.

In my 22 years of life, I have been inspired by many different examples of leadership, specifically through the students I have met at St. Thomas. In my time here, our school has faced issues of racism and sexism, and the response of our student body always amazes me. Students have organized and led rallies, teach-ins, and protests to educate and protect the rights of everyone at this school, so that everyone has the ability to have a safe, welcoming learning environment. My time at the University of St. Thomas has shown me that everyone has the potential to be a leader and to make a change, and I am extremely privileged to have had this experience and to be able to move to the next part of my life after having learned so much in my time here that will better enable me to be a leader for social justice

World Savvy:
Creating Globally Competent Students
Emma Smith

"If we are to teach real peace in this world, and if we are to carry on a real war against war, we shall have to begin with the children."
- Mahatma Gandhi

Story

On September 11th, 2001, Madiha Murshed woke up as a graduate student in New York City. Little did she know that September 11th would forever change her and her beloved city in such a negative way. In the aftermath of that disastrous day, Madiha began to be treated differently. Her Middle Eastern appearance motivated extreme acts of xenophobia against her. Madiha was seen for her appearance and was assumed to be a terrorist because she didn't look white or stereotypically American. This negative reaction from people who didn't know her at all caused distress for Madiha, as well as her friend and classmate Dana Mortenson. Madiha and Dana noticed the levels of xenophobia were rising across the city, affecting an entire community of hardworking Americans. In a moment of United States' history that called for love, unity, and understanding more than ever, the levels of hate and the fear of differences were rising exponentially.

The world around Madiha and Dana was changing. 9/11 proved that in a raw way, a way that included violence and hatred. This event sparked the still-warm embers of confusion and spite that have been between people of different religions and races in the United States for hundreds of years. Madiha and Dana linked the problematic reactions of Americans post-9/11 to their education; they noticed Americans' general knowledge of an ever-changing, connected world was lacking. The aftermath of 9/11 was a prime example of this lack of general knowledge about the world; Americans didn't know how to deal with the terror it experienced, so it began to blame anyone who didn't fill the role of white-passing and Christian.

Rising xenophobia wasn't the only effect of the lack of knowledge about an ever-changing world. Madiha and Dana realized that global issues such as classism, climate change, conflict, and food security were not being talked about in the general public. The two graduate students wanted this story to change.

Madiha and Dana wanted Americans to understand this interconnected world. They saw these global issues as needing a new toolkit to configure plausible solutions to solve. Madiha and Dana saw rising diversity, stronger forms of communication, and rising misunderstandings as an opportunity to change the education system. Both believed in education as a core element to any thriving society, so why not change what kids are being taught and how they are being taught so they can better address their changing the world?

That is exactly what Madiha and Dana decided to do. The two wanted to see more global competency in students' education so that they could learn how to make creative solutions to world problems.

World Savvy, an K-12 education organization, was created by these two innovative graduate students who wanted to create a better learning environment for younger students. Their goal was to create more global competency in an ever-changing world. Madiha and Dana wanted youth to understand the complexities of the world around them, as well as wanting to empower them to make a difference. Madiha and Dana wanted to equip students with critical thinking skills in order to address world problems like the one that Madiha and Dana found themselves dealing with in 2001. They wanted students to be able to look at a situation such as 9/11 and understand the whole picture and to not just come to an uneducated, irrational view.

World Savvy has expanded from its origin in the San Francisco Bay Area, to New York City, Minneapolis/St. Paul, and now in rural southern Minnesota and eastern Tennessee. World Savvy wants to help create positive change in as many schools as they can in order to create a more globally competent generation of students.

Theory

World Savvy believes in the power of children to change their world. The children recognize their power through projects and their imagination. Imagination is integral in a child's life; they are not afraid to reach beyond what is placed in front of them, looking beyond the limits of physical perception in order to reimagine the world as they believe it could be. This imaginative, creative, boundary breaking mindset is much more powerful than we think. So, what do children's imagination and leadership for social just have in common? Everything, actually; according to Peace Studies scholar Dr. John Paul Lederach, the importance of making space for creativity in the realm of peacebuilding and social justice is vital.

In Lederach's book titled *The Moral Imagination: The Art and Soul of Building Peace*, Lederach has four core disciplines that he believes to be of importance in the moral and imaginative peacebuilding process. The four disciplines are the centrality of relationships, paradoxical curiosity, space for the creative act, and the willingness to take risks. The core discipline that is incredibly relevant to World Savvy is to have a space for the creative act. The whole essence of this particular discipline is to create a structured space for peacebuilders to have the opportunity to think of new solutions in a space where anything is possible, much like a young child's imagination. Lederach (2005) explains that this process "requires a belief that the creative act and response are permanently within reach and [...] are always accessible even in settings where violence dominates" (p. 38). In the creative act and in thinking up solutions that go beyond current norms lay infinite solutions to global problems.

Successful social justice requires leaders to make space for the creative act; according to Lederach (2005), "creativity moves beyond what exists toward something new and unexpected while rising from and speaking to the everyday" (p. 38). The reality of living in a peaceful and just society is something new. The world is used to violence and fear being the norm, making the ideas and possibilities that come with peace and justice unexpected. Therefore, if we are to create leaders for social justice, we need to make room for the creative act. The classroom is a great place for the creative act to happen because it is already a setting that creates enough of a structure for students to be able to think up creative, imaginative solutions that will lead towards the success of the world they want to see. World Savvy is at the crossroads of believing that we should continue to allow children to be imaginative and creative throughout their lives. The traditional K-

12 educations system forces children to see the world as it is instead of how they could imagine it to be. The system is filled with tests and declining arts programs, oftentimes the only place that allows children the freedom to be imaginative and creative. Let's reimagine this system with creativity and imagination at its core. Children would continue to be allowed to see past the limits that the world has set up for them and begin to understand their own power to be able to continue to imagine and dream as they grow older, becoming more responsible, globally minded students in the future.

World Savvy sees and understands the potential that children have to use their imaginations to create solutions. And, what better time than childhood to show kids that they have the agency to enter into the creative space and imagine a more just and peaceful future for themselves? World Savvy opens up this opportunity through project-based learning. World Savvy's mission revolves around making children leaders for the future who are equipped to not only think critically about the world, but to also think of creative, imaginative solutions. Their mission states, "As the leading provider of global competence education, World Savvy envisions a K-12 education system that prepares all students with the knowledge, skills, and dispositions for success and active engagement in the global community" (World Savvy Website, 2005, np). Similarly, Lederach (2005) says, "Providing space requires a predisposition, a kind of attitude and perspective that opens up […] the spirit and belief that creativity is humanly possible" (p. 38). Lederach's theory behind the creative act and World Savvy's mission to create globally competent citizens is a pure example of how leadership for social justice is being taught to children through allowing them to imagine a more just and equitable future in which they want to live.

World Savvy implements creative, project based learning through their Knowledge to Action (K2A) plans as part of their curriculum. The World Savvy website (2005) describes K2A plans as, "an integral component of the World Savvy learning model that provides all students with a unique opportunity to demonstrate their *creativity, innovative thinking* and *drive* to convert their learning into positive action that has impact at the personal, local or global level" (np). Students' *creativity* is crucial to these K2A plans, showing that World Savvy is making a space for the creative act for these students to think of solutions that are beyond societal norms. The idea of making space for the creative act in these innovative, global solutions lines up with the purpose of the creative act according to Lederach, which is to think of imaginative, daring, boundary-breaking solutions.

The importance of the making space for the creative act is also vital to the idea of identity regarding leadership for social justice. Helping students and teachers form their own identity is at the core of who World Savvy is. Lederach's work supports something quite similar, explaining how important one's world view is to how they approach their work. He says that, "Creativity and imagination [...] propose to us avenues of inquiry and ideas about change that require us how to think about how we know the world, how we are in the world, and most important, what in the world is possible" (Lederach, 2005, p. 39). Dana Mortenson, World Savvy CEO, states how the idea of identity is quite important to those involved with World Savvy. Mortenson says, "We are starting from the student level and the teacher level, deeper exploration of their own identity and how their own conception and construction of their own identity [...] interacts with how they think about the larger community" (personal communication, October 20, 2017).

Creativy and imagination are at the core of leadership for social justice and children, so why not combine the two? World Savvy does that, allowing children to open up doors to possibilites that use their creativty to imagine solutions to global problems. World Savvy creates globally competent leaders for the future, and allowing them to use their creativity to do just that is crucial to the success of leadership for social justice. Children should have a say in how their future is shaped and be able to understand the importance of their imagination, an concept that can sometimes be lost in mainstream culture. These World Savvy students will be able to bring their well fostered imaginations and creativity into their future, continuing to imagine the world not as it is, but how it could be.

Action Plan

In order to have generations of globally-competent students, World Savvy needs to continue to work on taking action steps in order to reach more students and teachers. This action-planning and implementing social change, in this case in the education system, can be challenging; you are trying to change cultural norms and expectations even as you change tangible conditions. Therefore, social change needs to be seen as something moving, a plan that needs many dynamic objects and parts. World Savvy is a fantastic organization that needs imaginative action-planning in order to be effective. It also needs people, money, and resources. Conducting an analysis of World Savvy through the social change wheel, an object that has many objects and parts to keep it effective and moving, can be a helpful tool to envision World Savvy's future. By looking at World Savvy through the lens of the social change wheel, clear action steps will emerge on what they need to do to make their organization even more effective in implementing social change.

Below is the social change wheel, developed by Dr. Mike Klein. The seven strategies on the social change wheel are education, charitable volunteerism, community building, economic development/capacity building, voting/formal political activities, grassroots organizing/public policy, and confrontation strategies.

I see multiple strategies of the social change wheel as relevant to World Savvy. World Savvy is committed to education; that is what their whole organization is about. They have a strong model and formula which their educational and curricular practices follow. They are also quite good at grassroots organizing and community building, two strategies which go hand in hand. In order to have started their organization, they challenged the status quo and organized a NGO that challenged the current education system. World Savvy has built a community of educators, students, alumni, and leaders that all believe in the importance behind what World Savvy is doing.

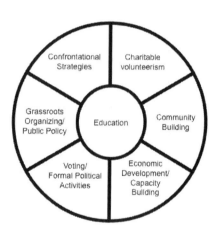

An aspect of the social change wheel that may make the ride a little bit smoother for World Savvy is the formal political process. I believe that working with education policy-makers at state and national levels could be extremely effective for World Savvy to try to make change at a systematic level. By lobbying and advocating for a reformed education system in America, there could be World Savvy classrooms, teachers, and leaders all over the country that are paid for by the government.

Another aspect of the social change wheel that could be beneficial is to have a stronger emphasis on economic development in neighborhoods in which students would highly benefit from World Savvy classrooms. For example, a poor, white, and rural school district who could benefit from learning about equity in the classroom and global issues may not be able to afford the training for their teachers to create a World Savvy classroom. By advocating for and supporting projects in neighborhoods that could benefit economic development for local businesses and families, World Savvy could have more influence in areas that would benefit from their programs.

The social change wheel is a helpful tool to use when analyzing the next steps for World Savvy. The future is extremely bright for World Savvy because while they have done so much regarding positive social change. They have so much room to grow and truly make an impact at state and national levels when it comes to the quality and content of K-12 education in the United States. As advocates for a better future through the education of our youth, World Savvy is taking giant leaps towards a more globally competent society.

Works Cited

Klein, M. (2017). Social change wheel analysis: Beyond the dichotomy of charity or justice, in Colon, C.; Gristwood, A. & Woolf, M. (2017). *Civil Rights and Inequalities, Occasional Publication #6*, Boston: CAPA, The Global Education Network.
Lederach, J. P. (2010). *The Moral Imagination: The Art and Soul of Building Peace.* New York, NY; Oxford University Press, Inc.
World Savvy (2017). Retrieved from http://www.worldsavvy.org.

About the Author – Emma Smith

I love all that is sustainable, vegan, and female-empowering. I first got into social justice/peacebuilding in my dad's seventh and eighth grade religion class and his lessons on Catholic Social Teaching. This has led me to double majoring in Justice and Peace Studies and Environmental Studies, with a minor in American Culture and Difference. I hope through studying leadership for social justice that my classmates and I will look at leadership through an ethical and equitable lens that promotes peace and justice.

Profile Assignment Instructions

The profiles collected in this volume were premised on the pedagogical foundations above, and structured by the assignment instructions and rubrics below. Students completed their profiles in five steps (A-E):

☐ Part A. Identify and Engage - Profile Inventory Assignment
☐ Part B. Describe Voice of People and Purpose through Story
☐ Part C. Analyze Leadership for Social Justice by Applying Theory
☐ Part D. Collective Action and Strategic Planning
☐ Part E. Synthesis

The assignments are included here to provide context for the structure behind student leadership profiles, and in the hope that they might offer ideas for other courses.

Part A. Identify and Engage - Profile Inventory Assignment

Instructions: Complete each section below by typing directly into this document. You can add lines as you type, expanding the length as necessary. Use the first draft to take make detailed notes, and the second draft to edit for clarity and coherence. **Bring a rough draft to class on [date]**. Submit a **final draft** via email in this format: **LASTNAME.doc by [date - one week later]**.

Objectives:
- ☐ Exploring key questions about your profile
- ☐ Confirming the social justice orientation of your profile
- ☐ Focusing the story you will tell in your profile - distilling a complex experience into a meaningful narrative
- ☐ Identifying a realistic and reasonable subject for your profile and anticipating issues of access and ethics

1. Leadership Focus:
Who or what are you profiling?
Given the freedom to choose any leadership profile, why did you choose this one?
What do you find meaningful in this example that you hope might inspire others?

2. Leadership Story:
What is the story of this person/group/campaign/organization/movement?
How does their **Story of Self** (individually or collectively) connect to a larger **Story of Us**?
Describe the identity of the person/group/campaign/organization/movement in leadership.
How does their **Voice** help you understand social justice in a different way?

3. Leadership Dynamics:
How does power operate in the leadership you are profiling?
Who is involved in **Decision-making?**
How is leadership organized (i.e.: vertical or horizontal structure)?

4. Leadership in Action:
What is the social justice goal?
What **strategies** are used to achieve the goal?
What **tactics** emerge from the strategies?
How does the mission align with daily action?
How does leadership work with other in **collective action?**

5. Leadership Context(s)

How does identity and social location(s) impact their work for social justice?
Is leadership occurring in the context of a local/community project, regional initiative, national campaign, or international social movement?
How are local and global work coordinated?

6. Experiential Resources for Profile - what access do you have to direct and indirect experiences

What direct resources will you use, i.e.: conversations, participatory events, art exhibits, protests, public meetings, etc.?
What indirect/mediated resources will you use, i.e.: mass media (i.e.: print, online content); proprietary documentation (i.e.: brochures, annual reports, press releases); third-party documentation (i.e.: documentary video, awards and recognition, academic reports, etc.)?

7. Consent Form

Submit consent form after reading to profile subject and receiving signature and date

Rubric for grading

- Great work answers most of the questions in all seven categories with detail, clarity, and coherence
- Good work addresses 2 questions in all seven categories with detail, clarity, and coherence
- Fair work addresses1-2 questions in all seven categories with limited detail, clarity, and coherence
- Poor work addresses only 1 question in all seven categories without detail, clarity, or coherence

Part B. Story

Instructions: Complete each section below by typing directly into this document. You can add lines as you type, expanding the length as necessary. Use the first draft to take make detailed notes, and the second draft to edit for clarity and coherence. **Bring a rough draft to class on [date] for peer review**. Submit a **final draft** in this format: **LASTNAMEpartB.doc by [date - one week later].**

Objectives:
- ☐ Distill data from Part A. into a story that gives voice to the subject of your leadership profile
- ☐ Construct the story in three parts: around a conflict, a decision, and an outcome
- ☐ Give voice to your subject's Story of Self, Story of Us, and Story of Now
- ☐ Identify ethical considerations about giving voice to your subject

1. What are the key data from Part A. that help tell the story of your profile?
Note the 7-10 most interesting and compelling data here. Imagine your data as beads of different colors, sizes, and shapes that will you string together into a coherent narrative.

2. Construct the Story - arrange on the narrative string of conflict, decision, outcome:
What is the conflict (injustice, violence, oppression or problem)?
What assets (skills, abilities, resources, ideas) does the subject of your profile bring to the conflict?
What decisions did this require of leadership?
What were the outcomes of those decisions?

3. Give voice to your subject (review Ganz, "Why Stories Matter: The Art and Craft of Social Change" and Lederach, "The Moral Imagination")
What is your subject's **Story of Self**? (See Ganz, and Lederach Ch. 2 for guidance)
How does your subject's **Story of Us** connect to larger issues or movements? (See Ganz, and Lederach Ch. 8 - On Space: Life in the Web)
What is it about your subject's **Story of Now** that is compelling for this moment in time? (See Ganz, and Lederach Ch. 3 - On This Moment: Turning Points)

4. Identify ethical considerations about giving voice to your subject
How might your story positively impact your subject?
How might your story negatively impact your subject?
How might your limited experience or limited research of your subject lead to inadequacies in your story? How will you address this limitation?
How might your own normative values color your story, positively or negatively?

5. Accountability

If your subject were to read your story, how would they react to it? How might their imagined reaction change the way you give voice to their story?

At the end of the semester, we will publish these profiles in a book that is publicly accessible. How does this public accessibility impact the way you give voice to their story?

Rubric for grading

- Great work responds to most of the prompts in all five categories with detail, clarity, and coherence
- Good work addresses 2 prompts in all five categories with some detail, clarity, and coherence
- Fair work addresses 1-2 prompts in all five categories with limited detail, clarity, and coherence
- Poor work addresses only 1 prompt in each category without detail, clarity, or coherence

Part C. Theory

Instructions: Complete each section below by typing directly into this document. You can add lines as you type, expanding the length as necessary. Use the first draft to take make detailed notes, and the second draft to edit for clarity and coherence. **Bring a rough draft to class on [date] for peer review.** Submit a **final draft** in this format: **LASTNAMEpartC.doc by [date - one week later].**

Objectives:
- ☐ To deepen your understanding of leadership for social justice by applying a course concept to your profile
- ☐ To analyze your profile in the light of theory to better understand the dynamics of power
- ☐ To add theoretical depth to your profile to enhance readers' engagement

1. Identify course concepts that might be applied to your profile (circle 3-5):

Stages of Team Development	Story of Self/Us/Now (Ganz)
Three Faces of power (Boulding)	Improvisation/Serendipity (Lederach)
Relationship of Identity/Agency	Hegemony/ideology (Gramsci)
Web of Relationships (Lederach)	Paradoxical curiosity (Lederach)
Pursuit of the creative act (Lederach)	Risking nonviolence (Lederach)
Asset-based approach (Kretzman)	Ethics of engagement (Illich/Remen)
Critical pedagogy (Freire)	Community organizing
Danger of a Single Story (Adichie)	Creative Tensions in SMOs
Democratizing Leadership (Klein)	Ethics and empathy
(voice/decision-making/collective action)	(values/duties/rights/outcomes)

2. Research your chosen concepts from our readings and your class notes.
Choose one concept that helps to explain your profile:
Story of Self/Us,
Describe this concept:
How does this concept help explain your profile?

3. Identify the key data from Part A. or B. that connect this concept to your profile?
Note the 4-6 most interesting and compelling data that connect to course concepts:

4. Using numbers 1-3 above, write a concise essay (2-4 pages) using your chosen concept to explain leadership for social justice in your profile.

- ☐ Describe your concept (with appropriate citations and references in APA format) - you may use sources from class and from research outside of class

☐ Use your concept to explain leadership for social justice in your profile

☐ Give examples of this concept in action through data you've collected (quotes, statistics, mission statements, organizational structure, decision-making processes, etc.) and/or your story (quotes, anecdotes, situations, questions, etc.)

☐ Conclude with a summary states the significance of your concept for explaining leadership for social justice in this profile and how it might apply to other examples (implications/applications)

Rubric for grading

- Great work describes the concept clearly with citations, explains leadership for social justice in the profile coherently, provides detailed examples, and concludes with multiple applications beyond this profile

- Good work describes the concept with citations, explains leadership for social justice in the profile, provides examples, and concludes with a single application beyond this profile

- Fair work describes the concept, explains leadership for social justice in the profile, provides an example, and concludes with a single application beyond this profile

- Poor work describes the concept without clarity, describes but does not explain leadership for social justice in the profile, provides a vague example, and concludes without clear application beyond this profile

Part D. Action Planning

Instructions: Complete each section below by typing directly into this document. You can add lines as you type, expanding the length as necessary. Use the first draft to take make detailed notes for peer review, and the second draft to edit for clarity and coherence. **Bring a rough draft to class on [date] for peer review.** Submit a **final draft** in this format: **LASTNAMEpartD.doc by [date - one week later]**.

Objectives:
- ☐ Learn how to use collective action models (SWOT Analysis, Strategic Mapping, Social Change Wheel)
- ☐ Understand your profile subject by addressing collective action, or develop a personal action plan inspired by your profile
- ☐ Engage on praxis education through exploration and writing, theory and application
- ☐ Identify insights from writing your profile, and limitations of your authorship, that raise questions about collective action of your profiled subject, or your own strategic action inspired by your profile

You explored your profile by researching it through Part A. You told the story of your profile through narrative in Part B. You developed meaningful analysis by theorizing your profile in Part C. You will address collective action and/or strategic action planning in Part D.

Part D may take **one of two forms**:
- Address collective action in your profile that reflects the profile's mission or purpose, **OR**
- Develop a strategic action plan for your own action that is inspired by your profile

Then choose **one of three collective action models** from in-class exercises (and accompanying readings):
1. SWOT Analysis (strengths/weaknesses/opportunities/threats)
2. Strategic Mapping (power relationships, allies/adversaries/resources/obstacles)
3. Social Change Wheel (service, community building, capacity building, political process, grassroots organizing, confrontational strategies, education)

Indicate your choice by placing an "X" in the box below:

	SWOT Analysis	Strategic Mapping	Social Change Wheel
Address collective action in your profile			
Develop a strategic action plan for your own action			

Now that you've focused your Part D Collective Action, answer the questions associated with your chosen collective action model on the worksheet below. After completing the worksheet, compose a plan for action in narrative form to conclude your profile.

For all profiles: What is your profile's mission statement or stated purpose?

1. SWOT Analysis:

What strengths and play an important role in collective action?
How might weaknesses inhibit action or block progress?
What opportunities are most promising for advancing your profile's mission/purpose?
How might internal or external threats lead to failure?

2. Strategic Mapping:

What key power relationships influence leadership?
What allies play an important role in collective action?
How might obstacles inhibit action or block progress?
What resources does your profiled subject have or need to advance your profile's mission/purpose?
How might internal or external obstacles lead to failure?

3. Social Change Wheel:

Which Social Change Wheel strategies are used by your profile subject?
Highlight or bold choices from the list below:
- ☐ direct service
- ☐ community building

- ☐ capacity building (economic development)
- ☐ formal political process
- ☐ grassroots organizing
- ☐ confrontational strategies
- ☐ education

What strategies are most significant to the mission or purpose of your profile subject? Prioritize strategies from most important (1) to least important (7) below:

What strategies are employed concurrently and why do they operate together? What strategies are employed sequentially? List in order, and explain why:

Finally, address collective action in your profile, **or** compose your own strategic plan, based on your responses to the worksheet above. Write a 2-4 page descriptive narrative (inserted in the space below, double-spaced, 1" margins, 12 pt. font, APA style citations).

It may also include a timeline of strategic actions, and one of these non-narrative elements:

- A strategic mapping diagram, or
- A list of SWOT findings by category (strengths, opportunities, etc.), or
- A social change wheel diagram

Rubric for grading

- Great work describes collective action clearly, connects to your story and theoretical analysis coherently, articulates key strategic directions for your profile or your plan, and concludes with multiple next steps and remaining questions
- Good work describes collective action, connects to your story and theoretical analysis in some way, articulates at least one strategic direction for your profile or your plan, and concludes with next steps or remaining questions
- Fair work describes collective action, omits direct connections to your story and theoretical analysis, identifies but does not articulate one strategic direction for your profile or your plan, and concludes with one next step and one question
- Poor work describes collective action without clarity, omits connections to your story and theoretical analysis, does not identify strategic directions for your profile or plan, and concludes with one next step or one question

Part E. Synthesis

Instructions:

- ☐ Begin your synthesis by copying and pasting your final drafts of Part B. Story, Part C. Theory, and Part D. Action Planning, into this template (see below). Add a brief (less than 200-word) biography by redrafting your leadership reflection from early in the semester, or drafting a new biography. Re-draft for consistent voice, and proof for spelling, grammatical, and formal errors.
- ☐ **Bring your completed synthesis to class on [date] for our final review.** Print one-sided (re-use or recycle paper if you can) so that pages can be taped to the walls of our classroom. We will review these documents (proof reading, consistent formatting, etc.) as a class. You may take this copy with you to make any final changes.
- ☐ Submit a **final draft** in this format: **LASTNAMEpartE.doc by [date]**.

Objectives:

- Synthesize a coherent leadership profile for inclusion in our class publication
- Decide on formal changes that help bring unity to the diversity of our voices
- Produce a professional quality publication that you can use as a writing sample for future professional, academic, or volunteer positions

Formatting:

- APA Style formatting for citations, works cited, and general format
- Format to: 1" margins, 12-point font, double-spaced
- We will decide on font and other formatting considerations in class (to be added to this template).
- Use the image below for the Social Change Wheel (do not re-size)
- If you choose to include a map, please create the map in a .jpeg (.jpg) format.
- Photographs must be at least 300 dpi resolution and in .jpeg (.jpg) format. You must have permission to use a photograph, and permission from the subject of the photograph.

Chapter Title
Author
Quote (optional)

Story

Theory

Action Planning

Works Cited

Author's Biography

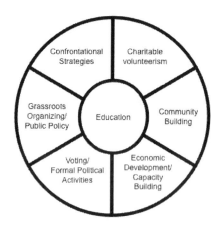

Index

About the editor

Mike Klein, Ed.D. is an Assistant Professor in the Department of Justice and Peace Studies at the University of St. Thomas. He teaches undergraduate courses in Leadership for Social Justice, Qualitative Research, Introduction to Justice and Peace Studies; and seminars in art and social change, historical interpretation for contemporary justice, and coffee as lens for interdisciplinary analysis. He teaches graduate courses on social justice pedagogy, critical education in social movements, and the pedagogy of Paulo Freire. His research, publishing, and consulting focus on: democratizing leadership, peace education, popular culture, intersection of art and social justice, and peacebuilding. He develops the agency of students and communities to transform structures and to advance social justice.

Also by Mike Klein:
Leadership for Social Justice, Volumes I - III (Editor)
Democratizing Leadership: Counter-Hegemonic Democracy in Organizations, Institutions, and Communities (Author)
Neighborhood Leadership: Celebrating Twenty-five Years of the Neighborhood Leadership Program (Author)
Teaching a Peace of my Mind: Exploring the Meaning of Peace One Story at a Time (Author)
Teaching the Compassionate Rebel Revolution: Ordinary People Changing the World (Editor)

Made in the USA
Columbia, SC
12 April 2018